POLICEMAN
IN
PALESTINE

Memories of the early years

by
Colin Imray

Edited by HVF Winstone

Edward Gaskell Publishing 1995
DEVON

EDWARD GASKELL
6 Grenville Street
Bideford DEVON
FIRST PUBLISHED 1995
Copyright © 1995 Colin Imray

ISBN 1- 898546- 05- 3

POLICEMAN

IN

PALESTINE

British Library Cataloguing in Publication Data
A catalogue record for this book is available from the British Library

Set in New Century

Typeset and Published by EDWARD GASKELL

FOR ANN
AND FOR THE PALESTINE POLICE

Frontispiece:
The Author in later life, sketched n Kenya c. 1950 by J. King

Contents

Illustrations

FRONTISPIECE
The author in later life, sketched in Kenya c.1950 by J King

BETWEEN PAGES 84 & 85
1 Colonel R G Spicer, temporary Governor of Rome, from a painting by Clemento Tavuri, Ravello, Italy, 1944.

2 RGB as Inspector General of Police, Palestine, 1932

3 Group of police recruits, Mount Scopus, May 1932. Author is third from left

4 Sports day at Mount Scopus, 1933. On left, Hon. Patrick Wingfield, later Lord Powerscourt. On right, RHC Taylor.

5 Author and wife Elaine soon after their marriage in 1941

6 The Palestine Police march again. Old Comrades Association at annual Cenotaph parade

7 Revisiting Palestine, author third from left, 1974

Maps

Preface

My original idea was to write down some personal remi-
niscences of RGB Spicer, who was Inspector General of
Police in Palestine during my own period of service with
that force – 1932/1935. I was then an 'Other Rank', but
circumstances were such that I came to know Spicer as
well perhaps as anyone in my lowly position could know
his commanding officer. However, there are others still
alive who served Spicer as commissioned police officers
who would of course have had much closer contact with
him. But so far as I am aware there exists no published
biography of the man, although in his book *A Job Well
Done* – a comprehensive history of the Palestine Police
Force – Edward Horne has published much material
about Spicer's time in Palestine. I must acknowledge here
and now my debt to that author. And on the same subject,
I thank most sincerely my old Chief's son PGB (Paul)
Spicer whose help in checking facts, providing confirmato-
ry detail and seeking out photographs has been unstint-
ing. For maps of Palestine as it was, I thank the Foreign
and Commonwealth Office and the Ministry of Defence.
For the transliteration of Arabic words, mostly phonetic
rather than grammatical, I take personal responsibility,
and for inconsistencies, which the reader may find irritat-
ing I hold up my hands. By and large I have accepted common usage as my guide.

Although I had no thoughts about publication, I found
myself thinking and making notes about that remarkable
man whom I and others had very much admired as a
unique and outstanding Colonial police officer. Then, by
the time I had got well started with those reflections, I
found that I was larding them increasingly with broader
observations on geographical, historical, and political
aspects of Palestine and the job of governing that ancient

land under international authority. Inevitably, those who served in Britain's Palestine Police Force in whatever capacity came to follow with interest, and sometimes with passion, the dramatic events which came in the wake of the League of Nations' Mandate; an ordinance which made Britain its steward and a small, numerically insufficient police force its protector. Just as inevitably, they came to study its history, to live with it and to identify with it.

Some years earlier, before committing my jottings about Roy Spicer and the Palestine scene to paper, I had embarked on a project suggested by a friend, Victor Winstone, whose own writings on the Middle East had given me new insights into the Arab lands and the British personalities who had played such an important, if hitherto neglected, part in their modern histories. HVF (Victor) Winstone is an established author, and I was much encouraged by his insistence that I should write down some memories of 'eye-witnessed' incidents during my time in the Palestinian Police. His splendidly researched book *The Illicit Adventure* published in 1982 by Jonathan Cape, providing as it did a detailed account of Middle East affairs from the 1880s to the peace treaties of the 1920s, convinced me that there was still much to be gained from a new and revised look at Palestine, where I could test theory, opinion and prognosis against personal experience. Accordingly, I set out to turn these random sketches into a unified story, though still from a personal and sometimes idiosyncratic viewpoint, and to give them the cohesion necessary to a book as opposed to a collection of idle jottings. I set out to reflect as honestly as I could the Palestine scene of those long-past years, and the purposes for which I and other young men were sent to police it in the years of the Mandate. I hope the reader may think that in some modest way I have succeeded in my aim.

Colin Imray

Prelude

It was November 1931. I was back home in England from Kuala Lumpur where I had made a somewhat tentative start to a business career. All the same, I had a job to which I intended to return. I was full of malaria and needed rest; then I would be ready to make my mark on the world of commerce. But slump conditions prevailed everywhere, and shortly a cable arrived telling me my services were no longer required. I was 'axed' and suddenly the world took on a sombre look.

After several months of fruitless job-hunting I found myself in the Long Bar of the Trocadero in Piccadilly Circus. I had gone there to meet a rugby playing friend from Malaya, Bill Galvin, and we soon found ourselves in conversation with a most imposing man – in size and intellect – who was clearly older than us, so we addressed him deferentially as 'Sir' and let him do most of the talking. His name was Douglas Valder Duff and he was full of Palestine where he had served for some years with the post-war Gendarmerie and then with the newly formed police force. Before Palestine he had followed a Roman Catholic education into the merchant navy at the age of 16, been torpedoed in the Bay of Biscay, become a novitiate priest, served in Ireland with the Royal Irish Constabulary and been wounded in conflict with the old IRA (quite different from the Provos of today), for which

1

last action he received a small pension. But Palestine, he said, was the place (I learnt from him later that he had left the force there under a fairly heavy cloud). We were entranced. It was the first and only time I met the larger-than-life Duff, who was to become the famous author of innumerable books and a well-known broadcaster and country 'gentleman'. But it was enough to send me hot-foot to apply for enlistment in the Palestine Police Force. I made my way with little hope of reward to the body responsible for recruitment, the Crown Agents for the Colonies in Millbank, London. To my surprise the reception was friendly and the visit worthwhile.

'Yes, we can offer appointments in the British Section of the force. Eleven pounds a month and everything found. If our medical adviser says you are fit, there is a draft leaving for Palestine next week.' It was all very uncomplicated.

Pronounced fit, I joined a draft of six and within days we embarked for Port Said on ss *Largs Bay*.

Duff in one fascinating evening of one-sided conversation had told me something of Palestine, of its deliverance not so long ago from the decay of Ottoman rule, and of some of the problems involved. I learnt too that in the police force there had recently commenced a transformation under a new and, so it was said, dynamic Commissioner. Few of the other recruits shared even my modicum of knowledge. We were raw young men, and there existed among us a mood of high adventure and 'devil take the hindmost'.

We were brought down to earth in the train from Port Said by a uniformed British policeman who travelled with us from Lydda up through the Judæan Hills to Jerusalem. In a short time he told us much that dampened our ardour. Even so, our arrival at the police depot on Mount Scopus was an eye-opener. We were barracked in condemned army huts, at the mercy of a band of very tough drill instructors. To such men as these strict discipline was the keynote of life and the first essential of survival.

It was on the morning of our arrival that I first met N O Lash, later, when serving in the Arab legion as second-in-command to Glubb Pasha, to be known as Lash Bey.

Norman Lash, an Oxford graduate (one of the very few then serving with the force) had suffered like the rest of us from the world slump. Unable to find a job he had arrived at Scopus on an earlier draft. We took to each other immediately. He had a most splendid wit that was a tonic for us all. His sagacity and friendly disposition became my bulwark against a world which at times seemed to me to be one of calculated hostility.

We soon appreciated to the full the kind of conditions that were to determine our lives for the next two years, which was the term of our initial contract, though when it was made possible to extend the term to three years I immediately signed up. Scopus was to become an institution that would imprint itself for good or ill on all our lives and it bred a remarkable camaraderie.

1

The Chief

I must come without delay to the man who was the very breath of our new life; our recently appointed chief, RGB Spicer.

Roy Spicer may not have been the actual founder of the Colonial Police Service. That distinction most probably belongs to the late Sir Herbert Dowbiggin, who served with the Ceylon Police from 1901 to 1937. He was Inspector General of that Force from 1913 up to his retirement.

All the same, it was in Ceylon with Dowbiggin that a 'New Look' overseas police service came into being, and its chief never failed to recognise the part played by his assistant, Spicer, in its transformation. Clearly the Indian Police must stand outside these thoughts; they evolved along very different lines. Herbert Dowbiggin undoubtedly modelled his force on what he called 'The Police Idea'; essentially the doctrine that policemen are in no wise military but are rather civilians in uniform, trained and organised to protect their fellow citizens from law breakers.

To Dowbiggin that was the fundamental precept. But his laudable idea was always up against the test of experience. And experience has always shown that the wrongdoer time and again compels the police to re-think attitudes and precepts, both to protect the public and to defend themselves.

Spicer, who had been at St Paul's school where he was

contemporary (just) with the young Montgomery (of Alamein), went to Ceylon as an officer police cadet in 1909. He served with the Carabiniers during War 1, was wounded, badly gassed, and won a Military Cross. Returning to Ceylon after the war, he served until 1925, when he was promoted to command the Kenya Police. In 1931, ten months before my own very junior advent, he became Inspector General of the Palestine Police. It says more for him than for me that he noticed me, a mere ranker, and that despite the chasm which separated us in rank we achieved a rapport which in the end was very nigh friendship.

Edward P Horne in his comprehensive history of the Palestine police force from 1918 to the end of the Mandate in 1948, *A Job Well Done*, recounts the events in Palestine that led up to the appointment of Spicer.

Horne recalls the anti-Jewish riots of 1929, and the explosive political climate. It was a War Office intelligence officer who adopted Zionism with all the zeal of the convert, Lt Colonel Frederick Kisch, who came to praise famously the rudimentary British police force of that time. After the August riots of 1929 he wrote a memorandum in which he said: 'during the period of active rioting and during the subsequent period of tension, it became abundantly clear that the British police are effective out of all proportion to their numbers in dealing with such a situation as that which arose on 23rd August last. May I say that one has only to come into contact with this body of men to realise how thoroughly deserved is the the good name they have made for themselves in Palestine.' Horne describes how Sir Herbert Dowbiggin was asked by Whitehall in the aftermath of those and earlier riots to report on the police service, and how – following that report – Dowbiggin's former Ceylon protégé, then commanding the Kenya Police, was summoned to Palestine. Horne also describes the painful, fundamental

6

reorganisation that started from the moment of Spicer's arrival in mid July 1931 following the departure two months before of the former Police Chief, Colonel A S Mavrogordato. One passage from Dowbiggins's report was readily accepted in Whitehall :

> There is only one matter on which everyone I have spoken to is in entire agreement and that is with regard to the good work and the good name of the British police....I doubt if the reputation of a British policeman stands higher anywhere in the world than it does today in Palestine.

With such testimonials, it is hard to believe that the force needed a radical shake-up. By Spicer's standards, however, it did.

We all called the new chief 'RGB' and I will stick to the familiar initials. His background, only sketched in the merest outline in his 'Who's Who' entry, is worth recalling.

His mother was a high born Prussian by the name of Adele von Besser, daughter of Baron von Besser of Powunden near Konigsberg. She met her husband Bullen Spicer when he held a professorship at Heidelberg. Her wish to marry outside of the Prussian aristocracy to which she belonged was frowned upon, however, and she was excommunicated with a small allowance. The couple eventually came together at the German church in London.

Roy Godfrey Bullen Spicer was born in 1889 and educated at Collet Court and, as I have already noted, at St Paul's. At the latter he was captain of school, of cricket, and of boxing. His gift of leadership seems to have germinated early. To his sporting credentials – which later on embraced riding to hounds – he added academic distinction, gaining a scholarship place at Balliol. After a term at Oxford his mother died and her allowance ceased. He was compelled to leave university and borrow the £100 necessary for the purchase of a uniform which qualified him for a cadetship in the Ceylon police force. He was a keen horseman and the discovery that the Ceylon force had a mounted section decided him on that course. He entered the service in 1909 and became a superintendent in 1915, when he was commissioned into the 6th Dragoon Guards, or the Carabiniers. He was seriously wounded in France in 1917 and won the MC in 1918. After the war, still suffering from the effects of gas and gunshot wounds, he returned to police service in Ceylon where he served until 1925, when he was sent to command the moribund police force of Kenya, a job which he retained until he came to Palestine as Inspector General.

I will not weary the reader with too much detail about the geography and physical make up of the force that came into being under Spicer. But a few facts, some remembered, some culled from Edward Horne's definitive account, will help to make sense of recollections that follow. First, Spicer took the title Inspector-General, rejecting the old title of Commandant as well as the home government's preference for Commissioner. Horne says: Inspector-General 'rang better in Spicer's ears'. That is certainly true. There was also an historical justification, however. That title had been used for many years in India, Ireland, and other parts of the Empire to indicate not only overall command of the civil police but also control of the secret service. In that capacity, the IG in India and Ireland especially, had control over all internal security, not excepting the very special role of the military intelligence gathering services. Thus in January 1933 at his own insistence, Spicer was made Inspector General of Police and Prisons, with two deputies, one in charge of administration and the other of the CID. In my day, the latter post was occupied by Spicer's old Kenya colleague Harry Patrick Rice. Under those two men the force took on a discipline, an impartiality and a sense of urgency which had to be seen to be believed. The Brigade of Guards became the model, as Horne puts it, 'for bearing and smartness'. There were no sacred cows, no one was allowed to have unquestioned ideas; and no one was allowed to question or disobey an order once those ideas had been aired and put into the daily routine. As for geography, it has to be said that our headquarters in the cold and unlovely old Russian Compound in Jerusalem hardly matched our splendid appearance on parade. It was a building to send a shiver down the spine of the policeman. The old Russian church remained in the quadrangle, and regularly at 4 pm the bells rang out. In winter the chill of the stone building was relieved only by smelly oil stoves.

Three years of relative calm remained before the storm broke in Palestine. It was during that period that RGB forged out of existing material the splendid force that would stand between anarchy and survival in the dreadful times that lay ahead. Our chief was ubiquitous, and our paths seemed to cross at almost every turn.

2

Mount Scopus

Such was the name of the depot about two miles outside Jerusalem where recruits of the British Section (then some 850 strong) were put through their paces in an initial three months of preparation. It was mainly a matter of 'square bashing', lectures in police procedure and elementary law. It was also a place of great historical significance, did we but know it.

We looked down upon the Old City on the western side. On the east – far below in the Jordan Valley – was the Dead Sea, faintly shimmering, and beyond were the grim Moab mountains where lay Transjordan, the twin Mandate with Palestine. Here it was on Scopus, way back in 70 AD., that the Roman general Vespasian, with his son Titus, marshalled his four Legions for the assault on Jewish-held Jerusalem.

The British Police recruits of my time knew nothing of 'New' Scopus, and little of historical Scopus. They only knew the 'Old' depot, consisting of a number of War 1 army huts surrounding a vast drill square. I arrived there in April, when the weather was hotting up and dust on the Square was starting to thicken. However, the nights could still be really chilly during that month. Our baptism on Scopus was quite an eye-opener for most of our small contingent. Here in bright sunlight we were decanted after a sleepless night in the train that brought us on the journey I have already mentioned, up through Sinai from Port Said. And at once we started to know what it was all about. The drill instructors were invariably ex-Guards NCOs, and they knew their job, which was to turn us into a disciplined unit as quickly as possible. 'New' Scopus came into being soon after I left Palestine for other pastures and it became the butt of rivalry between the aboriginals and later police recruits. The newer establishment consisted of four-man barrack rooms, modern washing and sanitary facilities, up-to-date cooking arrangements, recreation and study rooms – in fact, amenities that we 'Old Scopus' hands never even imagined.

It was at this time that RGB was weeding out a number of 'unsuitables', most of whom had joined the force after the 1929 Arab riots, and had been guilty subsequently of misbehaviour. They were sent to the depot and arraigned before the Commandant. Up the slope to the depot office would march prisoner and escort. A number of 'old sweats' would line the path. Soon there was the return down the path. The escort at the rear would make an undulating movement with his hand. This meant 'the boat' for the prisoner, a fate which the spectators would also indicate with exaggerated manual signals. It became an accepted ritual, but it was frowned on by officialdom and eventually discontinued.

One of the tribulations of Scopus was spared us fairly soon after our arrival. A troop of mounted men was based there, and the horses were stabled not far from the cookhouse. In that hot, fly-blown region tummy upsets were an accepted hazard, and there was always the danger of some fearful epidemic. Of course one could get used to that sort of thing, as to everything else, but it was better avoided. There were other equine problems. Every now and then a horse would 'go spare', and would gallop round the Square scattering drill squads amid a volley of imprecations from the squad instructors and cavalrymen. Anyhow, after only a few weeks the horses were taken elsewhere.

Then there was a hut known as 'The College'. This was

11

the VD isolation establishment into which periodically some luckless fellow recruit would vanish for a while, to re-appear in due course with a tale of woe. This place was presided over by a genial ex-'Black and Tan' known to all as 'Doc'. He had the biggest thumbs I had ever seen. I knew this from personal experience because he was also the 'boil' man. A number of us seemed to get afflicted with these scourges, and 'Doc' used to tour the huts and squeeze the boils, usually before they were ready to be squeezed.

It was a tough but generally humane and not excessively physical introduction to a rough and ready job. I recall that one of our companions who had been in the French Foreign Legion once returned to the barrack room in a state of semi-collapse. He'd committed a fairly minor infringement of the rules, and as a result he'd been doubling round the Square with his rifle at the high port. When he recovered his breath he opined that the Legion had been 'cushy' by comparison. And a large tough Irishman, flinging himself on his bed after a session under one of our drill instructors, said: 'I'll have a laugh and a joke with any man, but there's a limit to human endurance'.

And then there was the awful occasion when a man dropped his rifle (from memory I think it was Wally Meddler who was to die courageously but was awkward at drill). The corporal instructor, as always, said 'Care of Arms, Number One'. (I never did learn what 'Number Two' was). And then, from the corporal, 'If you'd been in my regiment, your feet wouldn't have touched the ground'. The guilty man was misguided enough to say sotto voce, 'Thank God I wasn't in your regiment'. But the corporal heard, and then of course it was round the square at the high port until the unfortunate victim was close to dropping in the heat of a Palestinian summer.

One of the great 'characters' of the time was Roy Fitze,

well known to recruits as a PT and boxing instructor.
I don't believe he was on the scene until about 1933-4. He
was one of the unforgettables, who taught us all a great
deal about the art of survival.

I remember also one particularly likable man who was
our law instructor. He was Sergeant Miller. He explained
the arcane details of the system Britain had inherited
from the Turks, the Ottoman Penal Code, and how this
was interlaced with the British criminal justice system
and the laws of evidence. Even at this early stage, under
Miller's guidance, I found myself delving into such
matters with increasing interest. Miller was also our
cricket coach (in the language of the late 20th century I
think he would have been called our 'manager'). He gave
us all a thorough going over in the nets, bowling a decep-
tive 'tweaker' I seem to remember. He watched us with a
hawkish eye in trial games, and advised RGB – himself
the most exacting of judges – on the potential of each of
us. Playing any game for a police force under RGB's
auspices was not a matter to be taken lightly.

It might well be asked how much in fact RGB knew of
what went on at the depot. I am sure that he made it his
business to know, and I often felt that he may well have
had a private intelligence system of his own. He certainly
had a very remarkable memory, not only for faces, but for
names, and the abilities, professional and sporting, that
went with them.

3

The Interview

My earliest encounter with RGB was when – with my fellow recruits – I was paraded in the corridor outside his office at headquarters. We were marched before him one at a time, and somehow when it came to my turn I gained the impression that he had me summed up immediately. There he was physically quite small, beautifully turned out in uniform, speaking quietly but forcefully in cultured tones. Alongside him, wearing three 'pips' was another officer, Michael O'Rorke.

Even at this first meeting I was enormously impressed by the chief. Here was somebody quite outside my experience.

'Is it your intention to make a career of police work, or are you simply here until times improve? I expect an honest answer.'

'I hope, sir, to learn to be a career policeman.'

'Good. We shall teach you.' He was clearly pleased.

'I see you were at school at Malvern. Played cricket there I suppose. What number did you bat?'

'Top half of the order, Sir; three to five, usually.'

'Turn your arm, at all?'

'Occasionally, Sir.'

'That's good. What sort of stuff do you bowl?'

I began to stutter a bit. 'Right arm, Sir. Off spin. Pretty inoffensive Sir.'

'We'll see. O'Rorke, kindly see that Sergeant Alderson is told to show Imray the ropes.'

'That's all', said RGB, 'I shall expect to see you on the cricket field.'

For me, this was the start of it all, the beginning of my career as a policeman. I still recall that meeting as clearly as if it were yesterday. I felt that I had been in the presence of a very dominant personality whose lead I could follow without misgiving. Even after sixty years, I can recall not only the things he said but also his demeanour and expression, like some premature video recording.

It was on this occasion, I remember, while we were lined up waiting outside RGB's office, that I had the first of several fleeting glimpses of another legendary figure of the Near East. Out from the office came a well-built, florid man in civilian clothes. There was a sudden 'Attenshun' from the Sergeant in charge of us. Then he almost whispered 'Peake Pasha'.

Peake had founded the Arab Legion of Transjordan after the war. He took part in the Arab advance out of Arabia towards Damascus on the right flank of Allenby's army that finally crushed the Ottoman Empire.

He was gazetted nominally as a District Superintendent of the Palestine Police, but his responsibilities in no way carried him over to the western side of the Jordan; his command centred entirely on Amman, and he was responsible solely to the High Commissioner of the dual Mandate of Palestine and Transjordan. However, this did not deter RGB from referring to Peake as 'One of my Officers', which apparently irritated Peake quite a lot. It was generally believed that RGB and Peake were never on easy terms with each other.

As for Dennis Alderson, he and I had been at school together. Sadly, as one of the very earliest promotional transfers from the Palestine force, he was shortly after drowned in an accident in Bermuda, while trying to save the lives of other members of his party.

4

Cricket

Some ten days after this initiation, it was announced that all aspiring cricketers were to assemble on the sports ground, as the IG would be present for net practice. By the time we arrived he was waiting at the nets, resplendent in white flannels and wearing, if I remember rightly, a Free Foresters' cap.

When he took his turn with the bat, it was clear that he was a stylish and accomplished cricketer. I was somewhat abashed when after a few minutes in which he dealt summarily with all types of bowling, I pitched a ball just outside his off stump and flicked his bail. I always thought my off-spinners were somewhat inoffensive, and could never understand why people ever got themselves out misjudging them. Batsmen probably thought they were too easy. Anyway from that moment my place in the Palestine Police XI was assured. As he was departing we were harangued briefly by RGB : 'I shall expect to see more of you men on the practice field; it is essential that the force has a worthy team'. Then he was away in his car, pennon flying, orderlies saluting, and the Depot Commandant standing to attention.

The Force first XI gradually began to emerge. We were lucky with some of the new intake. One of the early stalwarts was WF (Bill) Wainwright, District Superintendent in Jerusalem. At a later stage we were marshalled and encouraged by Laurie Harrington, also a District 'Super' who was for some while in charge of the depot. Then came

HS Swain, an Assistant Superintendent. He was from Kenya, and was a very useful cricketer, having played for Gloucestershire. Under the inspiring leadership of the chief, we all enjoyed our cricket immensely, even though the Scopus sports field surface left very much to be desired and fielding a hard ground shot was a somewhat dicey business.

But for me, there came one of those dreadful moments about which sensitive souls and ambitious young men have nightmares. I ran out RGB in a needle match. I can't remember who we were playing, but I do remember it was an important fixture. It was undoubtedly my fault. I called him and started running and then sent him back. Not the kind of thing a middle order batsman is supposed to do to a senior batsman with quite a few runs under his belt, especially when he happens to be one's captain and employer. I carried on batting for a while and made useful runs, but the sheer horror of my situation eventually got the better of me, and I was bowled. Approaching the pavilion with some foreboding, I found RGB waiting for me. He came down the pavilion steps, patted me on the shoulder, and said 'Well played Imray'. Later, when he caught me alone, he said 'Don't worry. It happens to all of us.'

The sports ground at Scopus during cricket matches became a kind of forum where RGB would talk in his voluble way, question us about our attitudes and ambitions and allow us to know him just a little – but always from a respectful distance.

He knew and was known by the great men of the cricket world, and he even seemed to be familiar with their families. I recall overhearing a conversation he had at one of our matches with the brother of the famous test cricketer AC Maclaren. I stood just behind them. It was all about his training methods.

'You see', I remember him saying, 'I have to train these young men to a point when they can face anything that may happen'. I did not realise at that time the significance of the word 'anything'.

I found the chief an inspiring, but sometimes over-enthusiastic and over-voluble captain. Fielding close to him, one heard many audible Oos and Ahs from him as 'Chinny' Fletcher, bowling very fast indeed, shaved the stumps or just missed an edge. 'Chinny', early on, had said courageously to RGB 'May I have Imray in the gully, Sir?' (where RGB himself liked to field). RGB slightly irritated, beckoned me to gully. 'Catch them', he said ominously as he took up position at mid-off. I normally did. I prided myself on my fielding in those days. I had good reflexes and was perfectly happy at gully. Incidentally, RGB always equated Chinny's speed with that of EA McDonald, the Australian Test bowler. I don't think he can have been far out in his estimate.

By 1933 we were too good for any of the local sides and had to look far afield for suitable opposition. There were some close encounters, however, especially when powerful army and naval sides came over from Cairo and Alexandria. We narrowly defeated the Middlesex Regiment who had a particularly effective bowler named Kennett. I remember the match well because I was top scorer with 18 and took four wickets. Then we had an exciting draw with the Grenadiers. I stayed at the wicket for an hour and a half for six runs, which the Chief thought a most commendable piece of fortitude. We very nearly had to eat humble pie when the Nazareth Divisional side bowled out a near full strength Force XI for very few runs. Again, I remember the bowlers who did the damage. They were Stacey Barham and Bob Jarrett. But 'Chinny' Fletcher responded with an even more devastating spell and we just won the match. One cricketer of real class who came through Jerusalem in my time was Hubert Ashton (later Sir Hubert) who was then with the Burmah Oil Company. According to Wisden he was one of the few batsmen during the 1921 season who had been able to play the Australian fast bowling pair Gregory and McDonald convincingly. I believe he never played in a test match. I can record, though, that he smashed the luckless 'Chinny' Fletcher all over the field. And there were even more distinguished cricketing names. Ian Peebles and RWV Robins both played against us for touring sides. Then there was AJ (Jim) Cassells of the Seaforth Highlanders, later to become Field Marshal Sir James Cassells, CIGS. The names, even the faces and the bowling and batting actions come to mind as I write, all these years after: Captain Alexander of the Gordons, a fine all-rounder who, if I'm not mistaken, became a general; Squadron Leader Steel of the RAF, and an excellent medium-pace spin bowler named Monks who subsequently played league cricket in Lancashire.

Our own attack was formidable. Fletcher, right arm and very fast, was supported by Harold Swain and Johnson, both medium to fast, with accomplished spinners in Woolnough and Marvin, and Penry Price's seamers; and if all else failed, my off breaks. Another excellent fast bowler who played only occasionally was Sam Peat, but he was stabbed and badly wounded in the Jaffa riots and never played again. As for batting, our openers were Good and Viall; the latter seemed to be able to read Peebles when that redoubtable cricketer played against us, and he gradually got the better of Monks. RGB usually came in at number three, followed by Swain, Penry Price, Frank Macadam and Colin Imray. My own forte was to stay there when all seemed lost, a prop for the middle order. Our keepers were the splendid 'Tiger' Watson and Jim Imrie, the latter enormously enthusiastic with a good eye and an agricultural method with the bat.

I must, finally, say a word about our ground. It was situated about 300 yards below the transport lines at Scopus. The outfield always seemed to be bedevilled by stones and it was the lot of a working party of prisoners, guarded in my day by Corporal Jolly, to tend the precious ground and keep it free of stones. Jolly was assisted for a while as a supervisor of the ground staff by the Hon Mervyn Patrick Wingfield, heir to the title of Lord Powerscourt. I remember him meeting his one-time batman in the 8th Hussars and the two of them getting drunk together. Jolly and Pat were hopeless stewards of the ground and the Chief was always on to them about those 'damned stones'. In any case, Pat wasn't with us for long. He married the heiress Sheila Beddington – from Government House. The Force XI and all that went with it was RGB's great delight. His pride in the team and its achievements was apparent and he would sometimes send the side down to Cairo for occasional matches against touring teams as a sort of 'thank you' few days' respite from duty. After my departure, the side became quite illustrious in the Middle East and I rather doubt whether I would have held a place in it. I missed the remarkable CAR Lawrence who, on a documented tour of East Sussex, scored seven centuries in eight matches.

5

Boxing and Rugger

An accident at cricket was to save me from humiliation in another of the chief's favourite sports, boxing.

RGB was just as knowledgeable about boxing as about cricket. He normally presided as a judge at the ringside and he expected all of us to take part, regardless of inclination or ability. My own initiation was nothing to be proud of. When RGB arrived at the depot he was handed a list of contestants, and he noted that my contest against X, a real Irish bruiser, had been cancelled. 'Why?' he asked.

'Imray has broken a finger, sir. We have replaced him with Constable Y.'

When he learnt that I had sustained the injury on the cricket field he was hardly mollified. He wasn't playing in the particular match. 'Misfield, I suppose', he commented.

'Batting, I think Sir', said the duty sergeant to whom he was speaking and who related the discussion to me. 'More than likely', replied RGB.

I had been dreading this 'Roman Holiday'. I had become resigned to the certainty that I would spend the next week or two with a broken jaw and nose, a lip looking like a melon, and sundry other deformities. I had even contemplated 'dirty tricks' by way of getting myself disqualified early on. I thanked the Gods when, two days before the contest, a ball reared up off a good length and caught the fourth finger of my left hand with a nasty crack. Now the unfortunate Constable Y had to take my place, and I was

21

there to witness the slaughter. Within seconds he was floundering around on the floor badly bruised and being counted out. I remember thinking with secret satisfaction, 'There but for the grace...'.

RGB would stand in the ring and publicly congratulate contestants after a particularly good performance.

As with cricket and boxing, so with rugby. The Force XV was outstanding. I can still see the amazing Bartlett at centre, weaving his way through everything; and the two wings Bruce and Beale outdistancing everybody by sheer pace. And there on the touchline would be RGB surrounded by a knot of HQ officers in kalpacks and blue greatcoats. As for me, despite a somewhat fortuitous appearance for Rosslyn Park first XV and some inter-state stuff in Malaya, there was no place in this formidable side.

6

Physical Training

There was a twenty minute pre-breakfast exercise; all part of the business of breaking one in and getting one into shape And so it was perhaps understandable. At the time it seemed an unnecessarily drastic start to a very strenuous day at the depot. Having passed out as a trained constable, the wretched recruit hoped he might be spared some of the rigours. But not a bit of it. Some of the men were retained at the depot. In my case I was employed at Police HQ for a short time so that I could continue playing cricket till the end of the season, but I was quartered at Scopus. A pal of mine named Heron Bruce had a job at the depot office, and all of us who were quartered there were supposed to turn out for morning PT. My friend, who had been in the place for some while, had contrived to get himself 'lost', and would sleep on blissfully when he ought to have been hopping around the square. One dreadful morning, however, a zealous corporal flushed him out, and the next thing we saw was poor Bruce in his red pyjamas, (they hadn't even given him time to change), doing 'small jumps by the front commence'. He and I had been out late the night before, and I knew how he must be feeling. Then his ill-fitting pyjama trousers fell off, and he was permitted to shamble off parade. I don't believe he ever got 'lost' again.

There was a sequel to this incident. Unbeknown to us, RGB had been making an early visit to the depot. There was never any knowing when or where he would appear.

According to his driver he had witnessed my friend's discomfiture and been vastly amused. Even RGB's enemies – and he had many – would always concede that he had a sense of humour, and could even laugh at himself.

Heron Bruce, incidentally, was another of those 'characters' who are thrown up wherever the British accumulate in any numbers. He was thoroughly idle (except when it really mattered), courageous, arty, humorous, and universally popular. He led an active social life in Jerusalem and knew everyone who was anyone, but he had no time for such mundane matters as sitting promotional exams. RGB, whose social life was very selective indeed (since he was sought in the most high-ranking circles), was heard to say 'There isn't room in Jerusalem for Bruce and me. One of us must go'. A few weeks later Bruce was on his way, gazetted to officer rank despite his reluctance to proceed through the usual channels. He was sent to British Guyana in the first place. Later on, while serving in Aden, he was awarded a police medal for gallantry. He ended up in Kenya during the Mau Mau crisis and was put in charge of a special duty team at Mombasa under my command, to the amusement of us both. He became a valued friend in retirement and had the habit of disappearing in the middle of a conversation and reappearing a year or two later, resuming the conversation as if it had never been broken off.

7

The High Commissioner

The chief of all of us, civil and military, was His Excellency the High Commissioner for the mandated territories of Palestine and Transjordan, Lt General Sir Arthur Grenfell Wauchope.

In the Boer War he had served on the staff of his cousin Major General Andrew Wauchope, marching beside the General at the battle of Magersfontein when the Highland Division was ambushed at Modder River. The General was killed and Arthur Wauchope badly wounded. He was mentioned in dispatches and awarded the DSO. In World War 1, commanding a battalion of the Black Watch, Arthur Wauchope was again wounded.

In 1931 he succeeded Lord Plumer in the unenviable job of High Commissioner, a post he was to hold until 1938. He was in effect the middle man between warring Arabs and Jews; between the Arabs represented by Haj Amin al Husseini, the Grand Mufti, and the Jews with the very persuasive Zionist Dr Chaim Weitzmann at the helm.

They and we jointly inherited the fruits of wartime promises which, without going into arcane detail, gave Palestine to the Jews with one breath and with another the whole of Syria and Palestine (excepting a stretch of land roughly analogous to the Lebanon) to the Arabs. In the immediate post-war years, the effect was incendiary. The balloon went up in 1920, on the day of the Moslem feast of Nabi Musa, or the Prophet Moses. It was an appropriate moment for the tolerance of the past to give way to overt bigotry. Moses being no less revered in the Judaic than the Islamic camp, the two communities were set at each other's throat by fundamentalist mullahs and rabbis in the shared conviction that they would go to heaven for their pains. The Jews were led by a man who had helped the British at Gallipoli in the war, a Russian-Jew in fact by the name of Vladimir Jabotinsky. More of him anon.

The Nabi Musa riots caused nine deaths, twenty-two serious injuries and two-hundred other casualties. But they were only one of many symptoms of an insoluble problem – the gift by a third party of one peoples' land to another. What essentially caused us all to be there was a festering quarrel as to the extent to which Jewish immigration into Palestine was to be permitted, if at all. Whitehall policy blew hot and cold, and Sir Arthur's task was the impossible one of trying to hold the balance between two irreconcilable nationalities. History has not been generous to him, but I hope that someone somewhere will make a proper record of his loyal efforts.

I recall two instances where I came into personal contact with Wauchope. The first must have been very early in my time at Scopus. There was an evening concert given by the police in one of the big huts, and many civilian visitors were expected. I was deputed to be one of the ushers, and was told by the Head Constable (senior warrant officer at the depot) to ask every visitor for his ticket, and to make sure that the front row was kept free for the IG's party. Otherwise I was left to my own devices. I carried out my orders with much zeal, but of course I was very new and very important-looking people kept arriving. Finally up the aisle marched a little straight-backed grey haired man, and I asked him for his ticket. It was the High Commissioner and behind him – hitherto unseen by me – was RGB. And RGB had an absolute sense of priority when it came to the relative places of young police constables and High Commissioners in the social pecking order.

'No, No, No! Imray.' I could just hear the chief's monosyllabic imprecation through the thick fog of my confusion. Then his sense of justice triumphed, 'Alright, I suppose you weren't to know'. I slunk to the back of the hall to be greeted by the Head Constable with 'You stupid young b- b- bastard!'. I stood to attention and replied 'Yes, sir.'

The second incident occurred at the Junior Naval and Military Club in London shortly before the start of the second World War. I had just entered the lift, when I was followed into it by the diminutive and now familiar figure of Wauchope. He looked at me intently. 'Haven't I seen your face before?'

'Yes sir, I was twice on duty with your motor escort in Palestine'.

'So you were, be damned. Have you a minute to spare? Quick gin, eh?'

We enjoyed a most friendly and engaging ten minutes or so until his guest arrived. Wauchope was reputed to have a prodigious memory, but he astonished me with that remarkable example of out-of-context recognition.

8

Lecture Time

In those days we had lectures and discussions and made notes and reports. The Seminar and Scenario had not been invented. And when it came to lecturing, Spicer had few peers. As a stage personality he stood somewhere between Lloyd George and Bertie Wooster, capable by his presence and delivery of holding an audience spellbound, and exhibiting at the same time a mannerism whereby he would emphasize a point by repeating a word or phrase, however ordinary. It is hard to convey the effect of his words at a distance of some sixty years. But I remember that on one occasion it went almost word for word like this:

'A young policeman married is a young policeman marred – yes marred. Years ago I was a young staff officer in Ceylon – thought myself a hell of a feller. One day my chief sent for me. "Spicer", he said, "I hear you're engaged. There's a train leaving tomorrow at 5 am for *Oojumkumshaw*. You will be on it." Now *Oojumkumshaw* was a place where no white woman was allowed. And that was the end of my engagement. The end of it you understand.'

Study, he always insisted, was essential to advancement in the force. By study, he meant learning *The Manual*. He would say: 'You all have a copy of the Palestine Police Manual. It was prepared for you by Mr Kingsley-Heath and is quite excellent. Regard it as your Bible, and learn every word by heart.' Kingsley-Heath was at this time acting deputy head of CID. He was a barrister, and extremely clever. Promoted later to command the Kenya Police, he had not long been in office when he was killed in an air crash. Many a Colonial police officer remembered him with admiration and esteem.

Again, the small, powerful, determined figure of RGB on the lecture platform comes to mind: 'You have to understand very clearly who you are and what you are.' Then came the bit about the Police Idea, and Policemen as Civilians in uniform. 'We policemen exist for two essential purposes: One is the prevention, and two is the detection of crime. Nothing else matters, nothing but the way we carry out those two vital duties. And, of course, our attitude to the public. We must gain and keep its respect. Yes respect. Unfortunately there has arisen a practice whereby the police are often saddled with a number of extraneous jobs that nobody else wants. This is no good, no good. I made it my business in Kenya to get rid of most of these nuisances, and I intend to do the same thing here, yes here. This is vital, vital.' As he warmed to his subject the repetitive cadences increased. 'Police must be free to deploy all resources towards prevention and detection. All resources. And how should we approach a proper means of prevention? We have to know When, Where and How our crime is being committed. Therefore, every Police unit shall keep a set of crime charts and maps. I have said just how these must be maintained and used. All this is important, very important. Believe me, I know. Thank you, that is all.'

There was a sudden crash as everyone sprang to attention; a passing gesture from RGB and he was gone. As I say, his dynamic presence and delivery were unique. Perhaps his effectiveness was due to an overpowering impression of frankness and sincerity, with just a touch of the *Boy's Own Paper*.

9

Tensions Within the Force

Conditions were such that there was always a trickle of wastage as men completed their contracts and went elsewhere. And this wastage was increased somewhat by the expulsion of 'Unsuitables'. Their places had to be filled, and it became known that since the arrival of RGB representations had been made to the Crown Agents that preference in recruitment should be given to men of 'reasonable' education. And so it was, and inevitably there arose a certain amount of divisiveness.

RGB was not always tactful. Amid the new intake of the 'better educated' there arrived up at Scopus soon after my own advent a certain RK Allen who had served under RGB in Kenya.

Allen was unquestionably a fine middle weight boxer, and the chief lauded his abilities. The force middle weight champion was then Johnnie Gammel, who was not only an excellent boxer but also a very agreeable and popular fellow. RGB had been heard to imply that Allen was the better boxer. This irritated a lot of people, and eventually a bout was arranged between them. It became a *cause celebre*, and the hall was packed with a very partisan pro-Gammel crowd. RGB was in the front row. I had begun to change my own allegiance by the time the men squared up to each other. Allen turned out to be a most friendly and unbelligerent chap, and I felt that he was put under a sizeable handicap by the chief's almost public declarations of support. As it happened, the bout was pretty even. Both men fought splendidly, and eventually Gammel won on points. There was little doubt but that he was the better of the two, but by no great margin. Allen's own modest bearing did much to overcome the tensions that had arisen.

10

Ramleh

Ramleh police station was said to be an unofficial officer-producing unit during the early Thirties. The historian of the force in those days says that those who were lucky enough to be posted there were expected to dress for dinner, and to become proficient in riding, polo, and all mounted activities. They were, says the same authority, expected to read, write and speak good English, be smarter than other members of the force, and have one eye, if not a foot, on the next rung of the ladder of promotion. Ramleh became the butt of many ribald stories spread by those not chosen to serve there. As one who was so chosen, I suppose the jokes went over my head. With four others – RHC Taylor, RK Allen, FT Macadam and M Holdstock – I was part of the first contingent of 'new look' men to be posted to Ramleh, but we certainly didn't feel that we were in any way 'special', and we did not dress for dinner.

What I do recall more vividly than our dinner apparel and our equestrian proficiency are the flies, the unbearable heat of summer, and the awful latrines caused by an acute shortage of water. We saw quite a lot of RGB as he was Master of the Ramleh Vale Hunt and we lesser folk were encouraged to join the pursuers of the only local prey, that friendly and gregarious creature of the Egyptian pantheon, the jackal. I wasn't in the mounted section, but I bought myself a shaggy grey pony which I could only afford to equip with a very old second-hand saddle and bridle. RGB, of course, looked magnificent on horseback, and his cronies used to come down from Jerusalem 'dressed to kill'.

I recall Stewart Perowne, then a district officer, who later became a Middle East 'expert' and the author of a number of books. He was married for a while to Freya Stark. Then there was Lord Melchett who took a very bad toss into some cactus. We had him in the police station afterwards, with several of us pulling spikes out of him. My hunting experience with this sort of company was limited. With my humble equipage I felt it better to keep out of sight. Alas, on one occasion, just as I was making a quick get away, I came round a corner straight in front of RGB. Eyeing me and my nag up and down, he looked unbelieving and said 'What is that you are sitting on, Imray?' There was, when he chose, a daunting hauteur about the chief. The polo field was another of the environments in which he revealed his natural sense of social superiority. Inevitably, he shone at that sport too. I never took part in an actual game, fearing for life and limb and for my self esteem. However we lesser folk did have a supply of polo sticks and balls, and we used to engage in some very unconvincing play among ourselves. We rigged up a jumping lane, and I recall that I learnt there to jump bare back. It was all good fun, but I really don't think we measured up to the suggestion that there was anything special about us.

One of RGB's profitable ideas was that British and Palestinians should patrol together and learn each other's way of life. This worked very well and one learnt quite a useful smattering of Arabic, though I can't say I enjoyed the eight-hour stints of plodding round the alleyways of Ramleh and Lydda. RGB used to say that after an eight-hour duty spell one must be regarded as 'dead' for the next sixteen. But it didn't work like that; there was the eternal kit cleaning, inspections, parades and court attendances – not to mention taking part in force and inter-divisional cricket and rugger matches. I remember being very short of sleep during that hectic period.

On one occasion at around 3 am I was alone on Orderly duty, which meant keeping the station diary, recording complaints etc., much in the manner of any police station anywhere in the civilized world. Suddenly the door opened and in walked the chief with kalpack on his head (the old Turkish headgear which was worn only by officers – never by British 'other ranks') and a police greatcoat over his dinner jacket. Mercifully I was alert, and had done all that was required in respect of complaints received. RGB however questioned me closely about them. Finally he said, 'Good, and now where are your patrols tonight, and what is their briefing?' I produced the necessary patrol map, and off he went to have a look and to inspect the men on their beats. He made a habit of that sort of thing, and would suddenly appear when he was supposed to be many miles away. Thus he gained respect and an almost mystical reputation with the force. I often wondered when and where he ever slept.

At Ramleh I had a spell in 'I' (Investigation Branch), where I certainly learnt about the use of the station records, and I watched the Arab Inspector and his staff at work. It was excellent training though, to begin with much of it went over my head. None of the staff spoke English and my Arabic was in the embryo stage. Accordingly, I decided that the best thing to do was to listen and observe, and of course to make sure that the essential records, including crime charts, were kept up to date – a neglect of which would assuredly call forth the wrath of RGB.

It was at this time that I made my debut as a photographer. I had to photograph and fingerprint all persons charged with an offence (and sometimes those who were never charged). I never became much of a photographer but I did learn a bit about fingerprints. All statements were taken in Arabic and it was my job to copy them in English. We devised a sign language for the purpose. But Sergeant Ibrahim, an excellent fellow who spoke some English was indispensable, and he was in constant demand. Our colleague 'Tackle' Taylor practised his only four words of Arabic whenever someone called out for Sergeant Ibrahim: 'Ibrahim Shawish mush hon', which meant roughly 'Ibrahim Shawish isn't around'. *Ibrahim Shawish mush hon* became a standard refrain in our living quarters. 'Tackle' was another of our more dashing lads. He came to us as an ex-RAF officer who had spilled too many aircraft out of the air for the liking of his seniors, and he was encouraged to seek another career. In the end, he found police work as inimical as flying. I believe he became a successful businessman eventually.

Of our original batch at Ramleh, only two survived in the force for any length of time. Macadam was gazetted into the Arab Legion and was soon to be killed on active service, dealing with a ghazzu or raid by Arab tribesmen. I passed out as a junior officer and went in due course to the Gold Coast. Allen stayed with us for a few months before returning to Kenya to join the Kakamegga gold rush; but he failed to find any gold and was compelled to rejoin the Kenya Police. If we were, in fact, specially chosen for possible promotion, we were certainly not the *crème de la crème*. There was a select and very special band of officer candidates who were destined for great things within the force. But they were certainly not 'Ramleh Boys'.

35

11

An Inspection

A divisional inspection by RGB was an awe-inspiring business. He knew every phase of the job far better than anybody else, and he turned the entire establishment inside out. So of course it was quite useless to try to pull the wool over his eyes or to evade an issue, as some misguided recruits tried to do in the early stages of their apprenticeship.

The Chief could spot at once any subterfuge, and was merciless with the offender. 'Honesty is what I expect, and honesty is what I intend to have' he would say, and he seldom had to make the declaration a second time.

I remember an RGB inspection at Ramleh. It covered the entire four-station division and lasted for three days. I never forgot what I then learnt, and I was grateful years later when in other territories I had to do my own inspections. This time the event got off to a somewhat inauspicious start. Incredibly, the punctilious chief had not turned up an hour and a half after his ETA. By then everything, including the horses, had been chamfered to the nth degree. At that late moment, someone discovered that there were no divisional crime charts and maps. Ramleh Station affairs were happily in order. It was possible to tell at a glance how, where and when our local crime was committed, and just how we were deploying our resources to deal with it.

But RGB expected a universal appraisal and our Assistant Superintendent had no 'see-at-a-glance' means of knowing the state of his Divisional crime as a whole, embracing four stations. How were we to get our immediate boss out of his difficulty? We all knew that to attempt to dissemble would be disastrous. As it happened our ASP (Assistant Superintendent of Police) was Bob Worsley, a kindly man if ever there was one, with an impressive war record and a most attractive wife who, we suspected, pushed him along the road to preferment rather more vigorously than he wished. The non-existent Divisional Crime Charts loomed over us like the sword of Damocles.

We had with us at that time a Head Constable by the name of Higgins, a delightful, rubicund, rather portly Irishman known to all as 'Ead 'Iggins. Administrative matters such as Divisional Crime Charts were his responsibility. He hadn't bothered about them, however, and Bob Worsley had neglected to push him. It was a state of affairs that was unlikely to be viewed sympathetically by the Chief. Higgins spent the remaining ninety minutes before Inspection rushing up and down stairs with borrowed graph paper, pins and coloured pencils, while the ASP was on the phone to one station after another trying to get statistics out of them. But we all knew in our hearts that it was hopeless. Bob Worsley had a habit in moments of crisis of tugging his moustache with one hand while slapping his leg with the cane which he held in the other. He was engaged in that bizarre act, I recall, when he and Higgins decided between them that they had no choice but to own up to an oversight and face the music. As the hands of the clock approached the critical hour, Worsley standing at the ready at the station entrance, there was a sudden earth-shaking crash. 'Ead 'Iggins, rushing down stairs after clearing away the pathetic evidence of his attempt to construct last-minute wall charts, had tripped and fallen headlong to the ground. He lay in a pool of blood. At that moment, several minutes before time, RGB plus his entourage came through the main door. The scene was made even more deplorable by the fact that Higgins had spat out broken teeth which one of the constables, RHC ('Tackle') Taylor, was trying desperately to sweep out of sight. RGB was not put out by his unaccustomed welcome. He told his orderly to take Higgins to the old Turkish hospital nearby and carried on as if nothing had happened. We, of course, never discovered how poor Bob Worsley fared with regard to the crime charts.

We were all interviewed individually, and when it came to my turn I was congratulated on passing my prelims in Arabic but had to admit failing my proficiency exam. 'Why did you fail?' asked the Chief. I explained that I had not memorised the manual sufficiently. 'I shall expect you to pass next time', he said. Then, as I saluted and prepared to about-turn, he said 'How much did you pay for that grey pony of yours?' 'Eight pounds, Sir', I replied. 'Feed it well, you'll get double that when you come to sell it.' I thought it was his parting shot. But it wasn't. 'I suggest you put in some bowling practice before the next fixture. Length and line were all haywire in the last game.'

'Yes, Sir. Thank you.'

12

Camaraderie

Thinking about it, I'm not at all sure that we made full use of our opportunities to get to know our fellow policemen in the Palestinian section. This was made up collectively of Arabs and Jews, and they served mainly in their own areas. Ramleh was an Arab area, and so – to the best of my recollection – most of our Palestinian comrades were Arabs.

We were quartered above the police station and lock-up (we were, of course, both police and prisons). The British were on one side, and the Palestinians on the other. However I don't think there was much mixing between us, except when RK ('Baa') Allen was with us. He was immensely popular with the Palestinians and although he couldn't speak a word of Arabic he taught several of them the art of boxing. He had a most infectious personality and his braying laugh – for which he was nicknamed 'Baa' – always kept Arab colleagues in stitches; they were often to be found rolling all over the place in helpless fits of laughter. Years after I knew him in Palestine, I met this likeable buccaneer in Africa. He came down to Mombasa to recuperate after being badly speared on the Kenya/Abyssinia frontier. When I asked him about the affair he said of his assailant, 'Oh he was a good lad, but mischievous'. I never discovered what actually happened. He must have been married for I met his son, of whom he was very proud, but I never saw or heard of his wife. He must have been an awful husband. The last time I ever saw him was in London where we had a few drinks together. He saw a column of smoke rising above the roof tops and exclaimed 'Good heavens, Claridges is on fire!'. He went off to have a look (there were no news reports of a fire at Claridges or anywhere else that night) and I never saw him again. Soon after our night out he was killed in a road accident.

The Chief had, of course, done his best to promote camaraderie with his policy of a Briton and a Palestinian doing patrol duty together, and this certainly paid off. And for me, whilst in the 'I' branch, there was daily contact with our indigenous colleagues. Looking back, however, I think we could have done better by way of fostering a truly international spirit. I think perhaps the mounted British police got closer to the Palestinians than the rest of us. They had a system called 'Sakinet' patrol. A British and a Palestinian would set out together on their horses to patrol a number of villages. Sometimes they would be away for two or three days, sleeping in the village 'guest house', usually infested with bugs, and eating Arab food. Allen, Macadam and Holdstock (who had been a sheep farmer in Patagonia) were among the mounted men. Their way of life certainly brought them into close communion with their Arab colleagues.

13

A Glimpse of History

In order to further my Arabic I used to walk up to Ramleh village and sit in a coffee shop and listen to the elders. They were very courteous to me; they knew what I was about and helped me a great deal.

Among our coterie was one very black-skinned and grizzled old gentleman called Abdul. I should remark that in Arabic there can be no such name – he must be 'Abdul-Something' – but that was the solecism by which he was known and it is the best I can do. In due course, and gradually, I learnt his history. He was in fact African, and had been born well before the turn of the century at a place called Wa in the Northern Territories of the Gold Coast. The slave-raiding situation at that time appears to have been that there were certain native bosses of the 'racket', each with his own territorial sphere of influence. Throughout a large slice of West Africa, the king of the trade was a freebooting rascal called Samori. His method was to collect villagers wherever he could find them, and then march them in manacles half way across Africa to an arranged rendezvous. Here they would be handed over to the followers of the notorious Tippoo Tib (Muhammed bin Said) who was boss of the East and Central slave raiding fraternity.

In due course the cavalcade would arrive at the big slave mart in Zanzibar, where further profitable exchanges would take place. I believe that if slaves were taken north towards the Gulf, a tribute had to be paid to one Zubeir, who seems to have controlled most of the slave territory of the Sudan and Somalia. Of course most African villagers lived permanently in a state of fear, and it was said that there were always 'monitor birds', pickets whose job it was to spot the approach of slave raiders and to give the alarm. My friend Abdul, in his village near Wa, had been 'jumped' when a boy by Samori's people, herded across Africa, sold in Zanzibar, and then taken by dhow up to the Persian Gulf. His fortunes then revived temporarily. He fell in with a humane master, and became his business factotum throughout the Gulf area. However, with the advent of World War One, Abdul was eventually 'jumped' for a second time by a Turkish army recruiting party. Impressed into the Turkish army, he fought against the British at Gaza, where he was taken prisoner. He then changed sides and fought against the Turks. Finally, after the war he settled down in Ramleh. I lost touch with him, but I often wonder if he was perhaps forced out of retirement again when Moshe Dayan swept through Ramleh in '48 and deported most of the inhabitants in order to make way for Jewish settlement. Maybe he was dead by then.

There was a small sequel to Abdul's story :

Some 14 years later, I commanded the police of the Northern Territories of the Gold Coast, and I had a police unit based at Wa. I discovered where Abdul's village must have been; indeed there were elders still around who recalled the curse of the slave raiders. Of Samori not much is known, though I gleaned a little from *A History of the Gold Coast and Ashanti* – a monumental tome by Walton Claridge. Local lore was that he may have been caught and executed by the French.

14

An Interrupted Patrol

I have mentioned briefly my baptism of patrol duty, stumbling around the pot-holed byways of Ramleh and Lydda for eight hours throughout a seemingly endless night. The only relief to this purgatory was Turkish coffee. The Arab coffee bars stayed open till 3 and 4 in the morning and by the end of an eight hour stint one was positively awash with coffee, drunk quickly out of little round cups. But one was unable to linger because there was a check system; one signed – or put one's mark – on a patrol sheet placed at a given point.

There were probably eight or ten of these points on a patrol circuit, and the briefing showed at what time the patrolman was expected to announce his arrival at the point. An inspecting officer had a copy of the schedule. For all this, of course, one had to have a watch. I have known an Arab constable who hadn't a watch carry round an alarm clock.

Nothing ever seemed to happen on these patrols. I must say that in my circuit the burglars – if there were any – kept well away, and the crime charts duly recorded this satisfactory situation. But I got very bored, and seemed to be permanently tired out. 'Oh please', I would pray, 'let something happen'. And then at last it did.

On patrol one night with Arab constable Jamil, as usual full of coffee and approaching another kahawah, or cafe, we suddenly heard a scream and a general hubbub.

Turning a corner quickly we were just in time to see a figure disappearing at speed round another corner, pursued without enthusiasm by some 'coffee' people. And there lying on the ground in a pool of blood lay an Arab. Everybody was talking at once, anxious to tell the story, and hands and arms were in eloquent motion. An Arab when excited lets go for all he's worth with tongue, hands and arms. I was reminded of one of the first of RGB's precepts: 'Your first duty is to save life', and the injunction rang loud and clear as I bent over the groaning victim, manoeuvring him in a manner that would have horrified a qualified first aider.

'His name is Ibrahim' said Jamil, emerging with difficulty from among the would-be helpers, 'and he has been knifed by Hassan ibn Waled, his cousin'. What to do? A pad of filthy looking cloth was proffered by Jamil. I stuffed this into the gaping stomach wound, and bound it tight with a kuffir (head cloth), commandeered from the noisiest of helpers. And now what? I felt distinctly queer. 'Go Jamil quickly to the Mukhtar's (local headman's) house' – where was located the only telephone available. 'Ring the station, say what's happened, and that we need a doctor urgently. Say I've gone after Hassan.'

Wondering what would happen if I were to catch up with the knife-wielding Hassan, I set off accompanied by a number of the coffee fraternity. Mercifully in the event, Hassan had vanished. After about half an hour, inspiration had completely deserted me. By that time however Jamil's call for aid had born fruit, and official wheels were in motion. Ibrahim in fact recovered, despite my first aid. He and Hassan, (who gave himself up later), had been drinking arak together, and had quarrelled over a family matter. And because the Ottoman Penal Code was relatively merciful towards this kind of thing, it was not long before Hassan was able to resume his place among the habitués of the coffee house.

15

A Near Miss

Muhammad Doshan was a latter-day highway robber and had been arrested and charged with that very offence. It was an act which, if proven, carried a long penal sentence. While awaiting trial, the prisoner was held at the fortress of Acre, an establishment famous for its ancient thick walls descending for the most part to the rocky seashore below, and therefore regarded as 'maximum security'.

Muhammad was a Lydda man, and thus one of our locals. Native opinion was that no gaol could hold him. He had escaped in the old days from a Turkish prison while under sentence of death. However, he had not been at Acre for more than a day or two when, with the help of a rope and cry of Inshallah! – if God wills it – he slid down those formidable walls to the sea whence he presumably swam to safety, or perhaps was met by a boatman. At any rate authority never again caught up with him, though it was not for want of trying.

Our CID section considered that as a Lydda man he would eventually return to the Ramleh area and Bob Worsley the Divisional ASP was instructed to leave no stone unturned in the search for him. The quest was followed with great interest, and indeed open amusement, by our coffee-shop fraternity, much to the irritation of a harassed police force. The kind of conversational aside which our informers reported back went something like – 'Oh yes, we know that Muhammad was here a week or so ago, but we understand that he is in another place now, though Allah alone knows exactly where'. It was all very frustrating. We were prodded constantly by the Chief and the Deputy Commissioner CID and poor Bob Worsley tugged ever more ferociously at his moustache and whacked his thigh unceasingly. Sending us on one wild goose chase after another became the favourite sport of the kahawah brigade. It was said that a 'book' was kept on our gullibility and that betting was brisk. Eventually, even the combined efforts of the CID, our own patrols and the local cognoscenti failed to give any kind of positive lead as to the whereabouts of Muhammad Doshan, and I can only suppose that he is to this day leading Israel's Mossad or some heavenly gendarmerie up the garden path.

One of the last gasps of this celebrated pursuit involved me in a near tragic accident. It all happened because most of the station staff had gone off to play in a soccer match and, since I was no good at football, Sergeant Hughes and I seemed to be the only personnel left in the British section.

AE Hughes was an extremely hard-working policeman. Indeed, when he died a few years later it was said that over work was the cause. One of his many fetching idiosyncrasies was a difficulty with his aspirates, and thus – like 'Ead 'Iggins – he was duly stuck with a nickname. In the case of Hughes he was known behind his back as 'Hay Hee', having been overheard announcing himself on the phone with 'This is Sergeant Hay Hee 'Ughes'. He loved dressing up whenever he could find an excuse for doing so. He prided himself on his Arabic, and often passed himself off as an Arab 'peasant'. And he was capable of the odd malapropism; he had been heard to say that he was sometimes mistaken for a 'pheasant'.

Our 'coffee-shop' informants came up with the suggestion that a profitable time might be spent by us in some olive groves not far from Ramleh, and it was intimated by an 'informer' that Muhammed might perhaps be found hiding in an old shack in the midst of the trees, for of a certainty he had been seen in that vicinity. The Sergeant and I arrayed ourselves in Arab clothes, though unfortunately he forgot to change his police boots. As we left the station he handed me a revolver.

I had been trained in the use of the Webley revolver. The drill was to load the six-chambered gun with four rounds; the space opposite the striker, and the space before it – on the clockwise movement – to be left blank. Thus, if the need arose one would pull the trigger, click onto an empty chamber, and then be ready to fire a live round.

On this occasion, the sergeant drew two revolvers from the armoury, buckled on one under his robes, and gave the other to me. Both guns were loaded as for the regulation Webley. Unfortunately however, I wasn't warned that my gun was a Smith and Wesson which had an anti-clockwise movement – and hence required the contrary action to the Webley.

The preliminary click would be onto a live round. I think my gun might have been an old War 1 weapon. (I did in fact check, years later with a London gunsmith who confirmed that the Webley and an earlier weapon which may have been a Smith and Wesson did have opposite mechanical actions.)

However, excited at the prospect of capturing the celebrated Muhammed Doshan, and experiencing moreover some difficulty with my unaccustomed garments, I did not question the mechanism of my gun. I don't believe that at that time I had even heard of a Smith and Wesson.

The shack was located in the olive groves. The plan was for the two Arab constables accompanying us to go to the back, in case Muhammed tried to break out through the crumbling wall. The sergeant was to bang on the door, and if necessary to push it in, whilst I covered him with my gun.

47

Accordingly the sergeant hammered on the door, which flew open; and there, standing above the sergeant with a heavy-looking lump of wood raised over his shoulder as if to strike, was an Arab. Fearing for the sergeant's kuffir-covered head, I quickly pushed my gun into the Arab's ribs, and was within an ace of taking first click on the trigger, when he dropped the offending balk of wood. The whole thing was over in seconds. Clearly, with my gun loaded as for a Webley, first click could have meant death for the Arab. As it happened he realised that he was the victim of mistaken identity and offered no resistance. He was clearly not Muhammed, and was only too thankful, when all apologies had been made, to be left in peace. He may not have been so understanding had he known how close he came to death.

I kept quiet about our near disaster, and left it to the sergeant to report on the existence in our armoury of at least one weapon with an 'alien' mechanism. Shortly afterwards there was a Force Order calling in all such revolvers and standardising on the Webley.

16

A Bedouin Raid

We had one other excitement at Ramleh.

It was about an hour after dawn when a galloping horseman from an outlying village brought news of a raid by camel-riding Bedouin.

The raid – or ghazzu – was an indelible part of the traditional Bedouin life. Any one of a thousand causes could lie behind a raid, which was usually a modest affair with at most a few injured bodies and some wounded pride. But occasionally it amounts to all out war and can involve generations of family or tribal feud, as in the conflict that had been waged for a hundred years or more under the Ottoman flag between the Druse of the Lebanon and their sworn enemies the Bani Sakhr.

Gertrude Bell, 'the Lady' of the Arab states, who travelled a great deal in those parts at the turn of the century, wrote:

> Between the Bani Sakhrs and the Druses there is
> always blood. There is no mercy between them. If a
> Druse meets an Ibn Sakhr, one of them kills the
> other. Now one of my muleteers is a Druse. He has
> to pass for a Christian till we reach Jabal Druse,
> 'for', said Namoud, 'if the Sakhr here' (my hosts of
> last night you understand) 'knew that he was a
> Druse, they would burn him alive'.

Not all nomads take it to such an extreme. If you are a Bedouin pursuing time-honoured custom and are

49

dissatisfied with the state of your worldly possessions, which means the number of camels, sheep , goats, horses etc. which you have; or, if you feel bored with life and need a change; or if you want to build up your ego; or if you consider the time has come to go and win back some of the livestock which somebody took from you some while ago; then in such circumstances you have recourse to a ghazzu.

The glamour and excitement of it all were splendidly recounted by the late General Sir John Glubb, another of the great figures of Arabia who was famously to take over the Arab Legion. To paraphrase his description: You collect together your immediate fellow-tribesmen and, mounted on camels or horses depending on your location, and armed with rifles and shot guns, you ride silently towards the village or encampment of your enemy. You arrive preferably at daybreak. And then the fun commences. With whoops and yells, and an aimless volley of musketry, you charge at the opposition. If surprise is as complete as you hope, you may succeed in rounding up and driving off with most of your victim's livestock before he has time to raise any defence. On the other hand you may have been clumsy about your intelligence and find that you have driven into an ambush. In this case you turn about, leaving behind several of your own people dead, wounded or captive, and depart with fewer camels than you had at the beginning.

Sooner or later your ravaged enemy – perhaps he is a near neighbour who moves about among water holes not far from your own circuit – will in his turn descend on you and your people, and the cycle starts all over again. And this kind of thing is governed by a fixed code of conduct. To injure, or indeed to admit the presence of, a woman on such occasions would be an admission of weakness and effeminacy in the male attacker which would make a laughing stock of him round the camp fire. For these people it is their 'Roman Holiday'; and on the whole not nearly so many people as one might expect get killed or even badly hurt.

Our affair was pedestrian by contrast; a poor thing indeed. The attackers were certainly Bedouin – probably from the Gaza/Beersheba area. They rode camels and possessed an assortment of ancient firearms with which they made a lot of noise and general commotion.

And there the resemblance to a genuine raid ended, for the victims were mere villagers living in settlements – fellaheen – and hence in the eyes of the true Bedouin, creatures of no account. But they possessed moveable items like livestock; and in any case life down in the southern areas of Palestine had become very monotonous. In fact it had never been the same since the British replaced the Turks. The latter had seldom interfered with the desert nomads, provided that all operations were carried on well away from the Turks themselves and the towns.

When the alarm bugle was blown, all available men paraded very quickly indeed. Spicer's new force already took pride in the implementation of one of his sacrosanct principles; speed of turn out. Quickly our Inspector, Townsend (known to all as 'General'), made his plan. He was on the spot, because he'd only just finished his tour of the night patrols. I myself had barely come off duty, and was still in uniform. 'Ead 'Iggins, to his chagrin, was to miss the entire party as nobody remembered to flush him out of his billet, and he hadn't heard the bugle.

The terrain around Ramleh is flat, interspersed with dry (at this time of year) shallow wadis, and a great deal of very prickly cactus. The Inspector's plan was to carry out a pincer movement with two squads of mounted men, five or six men per squad, cutting off the raiders from their presumed line of retreat. At the same time, two tenders (Morris pick-ups) of foot police would follow up as best

POLICEMAN IN PALESTINE

they could across the plain in support of the cavalry. Quickly I realised that my little grey nag wouldn't be up to this sort of rampage, and I swung into a tender. Regrettably the operation did not quite go to plan. As far as we could gather from conflicting accounts, the horsemen of Squad A, after a long detour, headed off a party of some thirty camel-riding Bedouin, plus a number of loose camels looted from the village. Unable to follow their homeward route, the raiders found themselves halted by a line of cactus. For a few moments there was deadlock. Squad B had arrived on the other side of this formidable barrier, and nobody could decide what to do next. The problem was solved by the arrival, on the raiders' side of the cactus, of the hotly pursuing Squad A. There ensued a brief foray with several of the Bedouin falling off their camels, and others being pulled off. A number of shots were fired but no one seemed to be hurt. Some of the raiders tried to make a get-away along a criss-cross of wadis. At this juncture one of the tenders arrived (I was among the occupants, still slightly bemused after eight hours of hectic patrolling around the Ramleh alley ways). The other tender was bogged down a mile away with a broken spring, its covey of police angrily cursing the driver whose carelessness has caused them to miss what they all felt to be the best day's sport they were likely to find in Palestine. There were still plenty of Bedouin around, and the action now became more serious. The cactus no longer remained the impassable barrier that it had seemed, and a splendid free-for-all developed with cavalry, foot-sloggers and Bedouin all taking part with obvious enthusiasm. There were some fine rugger tackles, with Bedouin and tacklers hitting the ground amid billowing, and none too wholesome, robes. After all these years I still have fleeting memories of 'Tackle' Taylor, riding bareback on his white horse, dressed only in a pair of shorts, swinging a mounted man's long baton, making whirlwind

52

probing thrusts into the middle of it all. 'Tackle' should have ridden with Rupert of the Rhine at Marston Moor, or at any rate with Chetwode in the great cavalry breakthrough in the Palestine of 1917. Had he been concerned in this latter epic, I feel sure that the illustrious German CinC Liman Von Sanders would have been captured. As it was, he only escaped by a hairbreath...... 'Tackle' was that sort of chap. I can also picture 'Baa' Allen on his bay charger. In moments of 'glory' (as on this occasion) or when inspired by a glass or two of the local wine, he would burst into his 'Battle Hymn' – 'The Cobblers Song' from Chu Chin Chow. And every now and then song was interspersed with his enormous baying laugh. And there was Frank Macadam, in full uniform, riding splendidly, in command of himself and all around him, as indeed he always was on the cricket field. Tragically, he was killed during an affray in Transjordan, serving with the Arab Legion.

How long our little encounter lasted at its height I have no idea, probably no more than a very few minutes. Eventually some dozen and a half shaggy-looking raiders were brought back to the police station, and a number of roaming camels were herded together and corralled behind the police barracks where, by reason of noise and stench, they precluded for the two or three weeks they stayed there, all possibility of sleep. The captives were charged under some relevant section of the Ottoman Penal Code, which had an appreciation of this sort of thing. An understanding Arab magistrate incarcerated them for three weeks each, and evinced evident pleasure that the rest of the raiding party had managed to get away. And on the whole the police engaged in the operation were inclined to agree. By and large a good time had been had by all. At least the monotony had been broken, and Allen was able to trot out a fair verdict, ' They were good lads, but mischievous'. Casualties were light; a raider had somehow or other shot off one of his toes; another, trying to knife a British constable, had been knocked out cold, with some damage to Bedouin jaw and English fist, and several raiders and horses, and at least one Arab constable, dressed in very little but his underpants, had fallen victims to the cactus, and needed much de-thorning. The only participants who were not entirely happy were the raided fellaheen, even though they had most of their livestock returned to them.

The story reminds me of how great military and historical events can be determined by matters so trivial that nobody could ever be expected to anticipate them. Colonel AP (later Field Marshal the Viscount) Wavell in his Palestine Campaigns says that it was the cactus more than anything that defeated the British in their first two attempts at turning The Turkish right flank at Gaza, where that wickedly prickly plant abounds. I have heard the same story many times. In my own Ramleh days I remember riding along sandy, cactus-hedged lanes, usually bareback and wearing shorts. A fall could be very nasty. The poison acts quickly and even though the spikes are removed the effect is felt for a while.

17

Some Local Leave and a Fracas

It was towards the end of my sojourn at Ramleh that I had a nasty spill from my pony, and also suffered a bad attack of jaundice. Released from hospital in Jaffa, I was given some local leave.

En route to Beirut, still a bit wobbly, I spent two days in Haifa, and went out with a colleague by the name of Robin one evening. We landed up, inevitably, at the Palestinian equivalent of a down-town pub; a drinking 'dive'.

Unfortunately the newly arrived battalion of the Seaforth Highlanders had just had their pay, and were out on the town in force. My friend and I were quietly going about our own business when, suddenly, our drinking den became bedlam let loose. There seemed to be several targets, my friend being one of them. A Seaforth wearing a bayonet drew his sidearm and seemed bent on assassinating Robin and, incidentally, me into the bargain. I managed to get a 'half-nelson' on the soldier, but my friend was being battered to pulp and I could do little to help as I had to hold onto my Seaforth for fear of being bayonetted. At that moment the door opened, and one of our constables put his nose round it. He just had time to shout some sort of admonition when a bottle smashed against the wall inches from his face, and he vanished. A Seaforth NCO was making valiant efforts to gain control, but blood was up. I was thrashing around with my arms full of a shouting, screaming Seaforth whose language was not for the drawing room. All he wanted was to get at me with his bayonet which, by this time, I'd kicked away under the counter. Eventually, a posse of police led by a Head Constable and accompanied by some military brethren shouldered their way into the melée. The sudden silence was uncanny. My Seaforth and a number of others were taken away. But poor Robin was badly bruised and had no further zest for fun and games. I seem to remember that the battalion was gated for a month. As for me, I continued up to Beirut, then the 'Paris of the Middle East', where I encountered an old school acquaintance, Terence, and after spending all my money on a night of folly with him I cut short my leave and went back to Ramleh. Soon afterwards I was posted back to Jerusalem and assigned to the CID. I hoped devoutly that RGB had not heard of my involvement in the Haifa business. If he did, he never mentioned it to me.

Henceforth I was quartered at the Depot. And from then on I became, willy-nilly, a member of the Strike Force. In the event of trouble anywhere in Palestine one was liable to be sent off to the 'bother spot'. It meant that you saw quite a bit of the country, but it did not mean necessarily that one was going straight into action. More often than not there were interminable periods of boredom, waiting for something to happen. You would doss down at night anywhere that offered, usually on the floor. Sometimes one got into an absent companion's bed, and was turfed out when he returned to his 'kipper'. That was the way of things for other ranks in the police service, at home or abroad. I expect it is more comfortable nowadays, and certainly better paid.

18

My Finest Hour

It was the occasion of the Ceremony of the Holy Fire in
Jerusalem's Church of the Holy Sepulchre.

The Rotunda is divided into a number of sections, bounded only by pillars, each of which functions as a chapel; and
by long-established custom these chapels are occupied
during religious ceremonies by the various Christian
communities which have the privilege of serving within
the church. These are Greek Orthodox, Armenians,
Latins, Copts and Syrians.

The Holy Fire ceremony, held annually, always gives rise
to tremendous fervour, and there is a progressive build up
of excitement right up to the climax, when tongues of fire
are seen to emerge from holes in the walls of the ante-
chamber leading to the Tomb itself, the supposed sepulchre of Christ. Obviously all this is contrived by a priest
ensconced cosily somewhere out of sight. At this juncture
the priests appointed for the task move around among the
people with tapers lit from these tongues of fire; and it is
then that hysteria is liable to boil over, and things can
easily get badly out of hand. Unless the various communities can be persuaded to remain within their own chapels,
there can ensue a wildly excited surge forward towards
the Tomb and the priests, in order that people may light
their own tapers or, very often, to allow the flames to lick
their hands, arms and even faces. It is then that denominational jealousies come to the fore, and old scores are

liable to be paid off under cover of piety.

From earlier experience, the Palestine Government was well aware of the implications, and there was always a strong police 'presence' in and around the church. On this occasion I had been posted inside the building, and was to control a bunch of some two hundred people within one of the denominational chapels. Briefing had been good; the details of the ceremony had been well explained, and even a short history of the various Christian sects had been given by the knowledgeable British Inspector Sigrist. There was to be no mixing of denominations; somehow, even at the climax, when the expected surge forward occurred and the screaming hysteria of some was infecting those around them, the sects must be kept apart. 'If they are allowed to mingle', said the Inspector ominously, 'one can never tell what may happen'.

And so, long before the appointed hour, the 'law' was in position. Converging crowds were marshalled steadily along the alley ways and approaches, and then into the Church itself which gradually filled to overflowing, each community filing into its appointed place.

We had all been paraded at dawn, and the hours seemed endless, but eventually all the stage-managing was completed; expectancy had been mounting all the time, and already people had fainted and were lifted over the heads of the crowds to safety outside.

With five minutes to the off, there was an ominous quiet. Then a sort of swaying undulation started up. I began to talk to my flock, nervously, in fractured French and Arabic and with copious signs. I talked throughout the performance until I was hoarse. Whatever happened, I told them, they were to stay put. It would be much better for them, they would see more and they would stand a much better chance of getting a light (or more likely a burn!) when the circling priest arrived with his tapers. In any case God would not approve of rowdiness. Happily, when the screaming and thrusting began, my little flock remained an oasis of peace amid the tumult. Soon there was a full-scale riot.

Even within the sacred precincts of that holiest of churches the police had to use their batons to restore order. I was quietly pleased with my small band of worshippers – and dare I say with my own performance. A few days later a member of the flock gave me a little carved figure as a token of appreciation. I have seldom felt a more intense glow of satisfaction.

19

Cold Steel

There were many incidents in those early days of the Mandate which were 'touch and go' for the numerically small police force. None rests more clearly in my memory than the day in September 1933 when King Faisal of Iraq died in Europe, and his body was transported by British cruiser from Brindisi to Haifa, whence it was to be flown to Baghdad for a state funeral.

Rumours circulated strongly among Middle East Arabs that Faisal had been poisoned by the British. It has been suggested that Whitehall Middle East policy had been forced into a corner by its own maladroit wartime promises, and there can be no doubt but that among thinking Arabs there was a strong whiff of betrayal. The promises in question were three in number: first, the Sykes/Picot agreement between Britain and France specifying British control in Iraq (then Mesopotamia) and Palestine and French control in Syria, with a codicil which gave to their Russian ally Constantinople; second the McMahon/Sharif Hussein agreement which gave in effect the whole of the Arabian peninsula and its surrounding states (including Palestine) to the Sharif of Mecca; and finally the Balfour Declaration virtually giving Palestine to the Jews. Suffice it to say that each conflicted with the other two and made the terms of all and each of them impossible to honour. Accordingly there were present at this time all the ingredients needed to provoke a most explosive situation. The Government of Palestine knew it, and very strong contingents of both police and military were drafted into Haifa in anticipation of trouble. The disembarkation of the body of the dead monarch, with its bluejacket escort – which was replaced during the journey to the small Haifa Airport by a party of Iraqi Arabs – was accomplished without untoward incident, except a very great deal of noisy excitement. But it was in the vicinity of the aircraft that a situation developed that very nearly engulfed us all in total disaster. The runway from which the RAF. plane was to take off was thickly lined by police, and a double outer cordon was in position around the plane to hold back the enormous crowds which had been flocking into Haifa from many parts of Palestine, Syria and Transjordan.

Estimating crowd psychology is never easy. Speaking for myself, I was always most wary of a sullen silence in a large crowd. In this case there was no such mood – quite the contrary, in fact; every man present (I seem to recall that there were few women around, a bad sign in itself) let himself go for all he was worth, with vociferous, endlessly repeated 'Allah Akbar', proclaiming the magnificence of Faisal, and cursing the British and all their works.

It seemed to me that we police were desperately vulnerable in that vast, screaming cauldron. Anything might happen.

Somehow or other the body and its cortège of Iraqi bearers were manoeuvred through the crowds into a comparative oasis within the inner cordon around the plane, where embarkation was almost indecently hurried. This inner cordon consisted of a detachment of Seaforth Highlanders under an officer, bayonets fixed. And it was while the pilot was revving up his engine that the floodgates opened. Disaster might well have engulfed us all, and ruined what was supposed to be a solemn event. The outer double cordon (where I was stationed) was broken everywhere by the milling multitudes, and police were at once overwhelmed by the surging mob, all thrusting and fighting their way towards the plane. Suddenly, for no obvious reason that could be discerned by the helmetless, dishevelled constables who had been virtually trampled into the ground, the crowd receded and came flowing back again once more like a herd of buffalos, and again our ranks were rolled over as if hit by a tidal wave. I know that I was on the ground twice, and that everyone seemed to be kicking at me in unison. But even as one went down for the second time under the mob, it was clear that the mood was different. Now it was fear that gripped the crowd – together with an urgent desire to escape. As the mob broke through and surged towards the plane, the Seaforth officer commanding the plane cordon had ordered his men to move at the crowd with their fixed bayonets. Clearly this would have been intended as dummy and not a real bayonet charge, but the effect was electric. I am certain that cold steel saved us from a desperate and potentially catastrophic situation. There were minor injuries, but no serious casualties as far as I could discover; astonishingly, even the media failed to capitalise on an event which had explosive possibilities. Certainly, if ever the use of this particular type of force was justified, it was on that day of the dead King Faisal's departure for Baghdad. And whoever was the Seaforth officer whose prompt action saved the day, many of us would gladly have bought him a drink.

Gradually the crowds thinned out, and by evening Haifa had returned to normality. Surprisingly there had been no fatalities or grave injuries among the police, though a number had to receive hospital treatment as a result of near lynchings. There were indeed many policemen who were thankful to be more or less intact after that mob stampede. Although there was never any evidence, there was strong suspicion that the rumour about Faisal having been poisoned by the British was spread quite falsely by Haj Amin el Husseini, the Grand Mufti of Jerusalem. He,

Haj Amin, was an implacable enemy of the British, and would leave no stone unturned in his efforts to bring discredit and embarrassment on the mandatory authority. Such rumours were as unjust as they were improbable. After all, it was Britain who put Faisal bin Hussein on the throne of Iraq, following Churchill's Cairo Conference in 1922. Enormous pressure was put on the government by TE Lawrence and Gertrude Bell, the great pro-Sharifites on the British side. Of course a man of the calibre of King Faisal was a valuable asset to British Middle East diplomacy, and his survival was highly important to stability. There was much press and cafe speculation, of course. Could not Faisal in fact have been poisoned (if indeed he was poisoned) at the instigation of Haj Amin himself? some asked. Faisal as King of Iraq was much esteemed by a very large number of Arabs. Equally he had not so long since been unseated by the French from the Syrian throne, and he had plenty of enemies. His brother Abdullah was enthroned in Amman as Amir of Transjordan. Those sons of the Hashemite King Hussein of the Hejaz (the part of Arabia in which the holy cities of Mecca and Madina are situated) were ambitious men, not lacking in self esteem or foes. On the other hand, Haj Amin, as his career seems to indicate, may well have seen himself as the modern Arab 'Khalifa' or 'Messiah'. He certainly viewed with intense jealousy the support which Britain gave to the Hashemite dynasty in the post-war settlements.

20

Footprints

Despite having attended a CID course, I was never very good at dealing with footprints. I found it difficult to arrive at the correct consistency for the required plaster of paris.

RGB appeared on one occasion just when I least wanted to be on view. I was in a shocking mess. Fortunately he was amused at the sight of the dishevelled constable covered by a nasty off-white outer shell.

However, footprinting did once enable me to help avert what might have been a bad miscarriage of justice. Jerusalem Rural CID was located in two or three dingy rooms within the old Turkish fortress known as the Kishli. It was built on the site of a very much older series of fortifications just within the Jaffa Gate – or the Bab al Khalil. When trade flagged for the CID amid these soul destroying surroundings, a deep gloom sometimes descended. And it was at just such a time during a particularly cold winter spell, with icy rain belting down (Jerusalem's rain, contrary to the popular impression, can be as cold as any), with most 'outstandings' tidied up, and very little to do except consider the awfulness of the world, that I sat and murmured 'How long, O God, How long?'

It was just the time to do some study. I was learning Arabic in a desultory sort of way, and here was an opportunity to put in some book work... But I wasn't, I fear, made of the right kind of stuff. Suddenly the telephone rang. It was Arab Inspector Nur-ed-din Effendi. His

64

English was even worse than my Arabic but we got along well enough. Nur-ed-din seemed to have taken me under his wing, and I was grateful. 'Please come with me at once to Jimsu village, and bring your footprint gear with you. I am waiting.' I picked him up and we set off. The journey to Jimsu by police tender took about an hour along some very rough tracks. Nur-ed-din Effendi sat cosily in front under cover with the driver; I was bumped about in the back, getting wetter and colder every moment from the rain which never seemed to let up. At Jimsu there was the usual coffee ceremony at the Mukhtar's house before anything could happen. Then Nur-ed-din, in the slow 'kitchen' Arabic that he used with me, related the story he had gleaned from the Mukhtar. It certainly seemed to be simple enough. A prisoner by the name of Hamed was triumphantly produced from a nearby pig-pen wherein he had been incarcerated for some hours. It was apparent that Hamed was very angry indeed. 'Regard this man's left foot', said Nur-ed-din, 'he has no little toe'. He went on: 'The Mukhtar says that Yusuf here' – he turned towards a smiling, obsequious, thoroughly unlikable individual – 'had his house broken into whilst he was away yesterday afternoon, and four of his goats are missing. And there has been fassad (dispute) between Yusuf and Hamed for a long time. But...' – here Nur-ed-din pushed his face into mine – 'there are footprints in flour lying upon the ground and leading up to where the goats were tethered, and' – Nur-ed-din's nose was now pushed Zulu fashion right alongside mine – 'those footprints show the lack of a little toe on the left foot.'

And so we proceeded to the scene of the crime, accompanied by the Mukhtar, complainant Yusuf and accused Hamed, still smelling strongly of pig-sty, and still protesting loudly.

Sure enough, there in a heavy spill-over of flour from sacks piled up in the corner, were some very clear footprints going left right, left right, up to the goat corral, out of which the wooden door had been pushed off its rickety hinges. And the left footprints showed very clearly that whoever had made them lacked a little toe. Everyone looked at the sandal-less Hamed. His culpability was surely beyond dispute. Hamed was more than a little sensitive about all this. He cursed loud and long, with hands and arms moving like pistons to emphasize whatever point he was trying to make in the Arabic that I was striving to follow, but which denoted very clearly a most strenuous denial. On this occasion I found little difficulty in dealing with the prints. Half way through making my cast, I found myself looking at Hamed's left foot, and then back again to the toe-less left foot print. Somehow, Hamed's foot seemed broader and longer than the print. I drew Nur-ed-din's attention to the apparent discrepancy. But having been nurtured on Turkish 'rough' justice, he would have none of it. Could there possibly be in the Jerusalem Rural District more than one man who had a little toe missing from his left foot? With Nur-ed-din and the Mukhtar going into conference on local affairs over yet more cups of coffee, I – just in case – made Hamed run, walk, dance and jump along what remained of the flour. The result confirmed my sneaking suspicion. The prints of Hamed, there in the flesh, in no way corresponded with those imprinted in the flour. But with Nur-ed-din obdurate, there was no point in arguing. There was no doubt about what had to happen. The continually protesting Hamed was arrested and stuffed into the back of the tender with me as escort. And here at last during the return journey to Jerusalem, the rain did what nothing else had been able to do; it reduced Hamed to morose silence. The case, so far as Nur-ed-din was concerned, was 'open and shut', and he was awaiting pleasurably one more commendation to add to his already long list for diligent investigation of crime.

But there was to be a hitch. I had spent a sleepless night and next morning sought an urgent interview with the 'Super'. I told him the story. A veteran from Ireland, and an excellent 'field' policeman, he listened and said he would look into things. In the meantime I was to assemble the facts and be ready to present the rebutting footprint evidence. For me this was to be the first of a number of occasions in my career when I was to be 'pig-in-the-middle'. I didn't want to let down Nur-ed-din, but what was I to do? And then mercifully, the very next day, another one of gloom at the Kishli, with Hamed charged and awaiting justice through the courts, there came a bombshell. With a smile of triumph, in walked the Jimsu Mukhtar with a story that was to shake everyone. According to him, another toe-less left footer, one Ali al Bedawi, had been found actually driving Yusuf's four goats away into the depths of the rocky hills. And behold, here he was, all ready for the Mandate police to examine this extraordinary coincidence.

With the lordly mien of a conjuror, the Mukhtar clapped his hands, and the wretched Ali, with hands bound, was kicked into the room by two of the village special constabulary. The true story then emerged. Ali was indeed the malefactor. Having been foiled in making his get-away with the goats, he gave no trouble at all. He had in fact long coveted Yusuf's wife, and had been hanging round hoping for a favourable opportunity. But whilst engaged on his reconnaissance, he had seized the chance – in the absence of Yusuf – to 'knock off' four of his goats. He had evidently resigned himself to the prison sentence he eventually received, and in the meantime was beaming toothily at everybody. I was curious to know why it was that he seemed to be so happy.

'Sir' said Ali, 'you do not understand. For years I had thought myself to be the only little toe-less left footer in the world, and now I have found that I have gained a brother.' But Hamed, restored to liberty and confronted with Ali, made it clear in unprintable terms that he rejected this fraternal approach.

21

Abu Jildeh

For some three to four weeks, the tall, straight, silent figure, dressed in the awful black and grey striped prison uniform, walked daily for his allotted hour in the prison exercise yard.

Finally, on the appointed morning, he spoke :

'Khatrak Kulkum Mahabis.' (Goodbye all you prisoners).

Thus did Abu Jildeh, dignified at the last, bid farewell to the remaining occupants of the condemned cells in Jerusalem's Central Prison, as he walked the few yards to the trap. Saleh Armeet, his friend and fellow gangster, was to follow him that same morning.

In the Palestine of the Mandate, both police and prisons operated under the Inspector General of Police, and inevitably it occurred that individual policemen were required from time to time for spells of prison duty. Hence they might very well find themselves attending the grim business of an execution. Some took the whole ghastly business in their stride, or so it appeared to those who knew them. For others, both before and after the thing happened, it was nightmare of the worst kind.

For nearly a year Abu Jildeh and his band roamed the hills of Judœa and southern Samaria, both north and east of Jerusalem. He was alluded to sometimes by those who saw only the glamour, as 'The Arab Robin Hood'. But though in the end he died well, there was nothing during Abu Jildeh's reign in the rugged Palestinian hill country that measured up to the chivalrous courage and daring of the Robin Hood of fiction. The only points of resemblance perhaps lay in the swift forays upon villages, the skilfully laid ambushes of travellers and police patrols, and the silent traceless melting away into the hills after each raid. There was even, on at least one memorable occasion, the shooting-up at night of the police depot itself, on the very fringe of Jerusalem. It never did transpire what Abu Jildeh hoped to achieve by this escapade in which luckily there were no police casualties. Maybe it was just bravado. Abu Jildeh was in fact a bandit in every sense; a cruel, callous bandit, and in the end a proved murderer. He had learned about banditry during the Turkish regime when, as a youth, he followed his father and brothers and took part in their marauding expeditions. His story was told in the Vienna Cafe during many an evening session by Assistant Superintendent of Police Abdin Bey. Abdin, an Arab who had been a policeman under the Turks, would certainly have known all about this sort of thing for his local knowledge was encyclopaedic. As a raconteur he was second to none. Thus, according to Abdin, Abu Jildeh had tried his hand at banditry up in the French mandated land of Syria, where life had been made too dangerous for him, and where his father and one of his brothers had been killed in action with the authorities. He had, therefore, set up business in the Palestinian hill country that he knew so well. He hoped no doubt that the British would be less aggressive than the French towards him and his kind. Abu Jildeh employed the usual modus operandi of those who have followed banditry and guerilla activity as a career. Basically he terrorised the villagers whose paths he crossed. He knew his ground thoroughly, for he was born and bred in the area. And the same applied to his second in command, Saleh Armeet, who had grown up with him. But they were probably the only locals of the entire band (apart from our friend Mohammed Doshan) which at the zenith of its power numbered some thirty to forty followers. They were mostly from Syria and northern Palestine. It has been said that several of these who later were to fight British and Jews indiscriminately, gained their experience of hill-fighting under Abu Jildeh. And years later, a former officer in the Palestine Police became convinced that Abu Jildeh might well have been mixed up with the Grand Mufti himself, the redoubtable Haj Amin el Husseini. It has been said earlier that Haj Amin would leave no stone unturned in his determination to undermine the mandatory power, Britain.

The band lived of course off the unhappy villagers, who were much too frightened to 'tip off' the police. Indeed there was sound evidence of summary executions of people who refused to help the gang. In the early stages, Abu Jildeh had been just another bandit. And Palestine had always been full of bandits, although since the British came on the scene armed robberies had diminished much. However, banditry was still common enough for the older officers to regard it as part of the days work. And so when a report came in that Abu Jildeh was in the vicinity, a police party would race along the road in tenders, disembark, and then advance in extended order, hoping vaguely to catch the intruder in their net. The sole result of this kind of thing was to provoke a volley of musketry from Abu Jildeh and his band, hidden comfortably among uninviting crags and cliffs. Fortunately none of the gang seemed to be very good shots. The police would dutifully return the fire, and then climb wearily and warily towards the place where the bandits had been but no longer were. In the event, everybody usually went home, footsore, browned off, and somehow rather ashamed. I had two experiences of this sort of thing, and once a bullet struck a rock a little too close for my peace of mind. But soon things were to change. Abu Jildeh overstepped the mark with the cold-blooded murder of a mounted police patrol. Four Arab constables, each carrying a rifle and full bandoliers, were halted suddenly at gun-point in rocky terrain. Their rifles, bandoliers and horses were taken by the gang, and they themselves put up against a rock and shot with their own rifles. Three were killed, but the fourth, left for dead, managed apparently to stagger back to where he could find help.

Abu Jildeh was to be taken very seriously from then on, and the full force of the Palestine Police was deployed against the gang.

The surviving victim later stated his belief that Abu Jildeh himself had been present and conducted the whole affair, but as no member of the police had ever seen Abu Jildeh, there remained some doubt about this. However, after his arrest the constable did very decisively pick out the bandit at a properly conducted identification parade. That was by no means the only testimony that finally sent the multi-murderer to the gallows. Indeed the evidence from a number of sources was overwhelming.

It was at about the time of the police ambush that the gang started to waylay and rob travellers on the roads between Jerusalem and Nablus, and Jerusalem and Jericho. A car ride along the Jericho road to the Dead Sea was popular at that time among residents of Jerusalem, and there came a story that a senior legal officer was forced at gunpoint to dispense his trousers to a member of the gang who liked the look of them. Money and valuables were always taken, and there was apparently a bad moment for a lady who found difficulty in taking off her ring, when the bandit threatened to cut off her finger. Indeed during Abu Jildeh's reign of terror, there was a revival of the notoriety of the Wadi Haramiyyeh (The Valley of the Robbers) on the Jericho road, dating back to biblical times. For the police it became a first priority to run the gangsters to earth. A massive operation was mounted against them under the personal direction of our deputy chief, Major Alan Saunders. Here was a very splendid officer who had served for six years with the Indian police before World War 1. Towards the end of it all he had found himself in Palestine under Allenby, and finally joined the Palestine police.

The strategy followed was common enough – progressive denial of access to the terrain where the criminal is believed to operate. An earlier example was Kitchener's blockhouse system against De Wet's Boer War guerrillas; and much later on in Kenya the security forces used similar methods against the Mau Mau. I was learning lessons that would be useful in years to come. I found myself taking my turn at village outpost duty. This entailed establishing a series of temporary police posts in and around the area worked by the gang – thus giving protection to the villagers and denying food and shelter to the gangsters. That particular Palestinian winter was I recall a bleak one, and the rocky hill country, so dry and arid in summer, with wind and rain now driving constantly over it, provided the best possible conditions for the police operation, because the gangsters were stretched to find shelter, except in caves. For me and my British companions, however, sitting wet and cold in a village (that smelt abominably) perched high up on an exposed hill top, time seemed to stand still. The forty-eight hour tour of duty which alternated with forty eight hours rest back in the Depot, seemed a penance. However, Saunders' leadership kept us going, and we were determined to 'get' Abu Jildeh. It was essential, moreover to keep constantly on the alert. News came in that one of the posts a few miles away had been shot up by the gang, a couple of constables had been wounded, some rifles stolen, a hut burnt down, and enough food pilfered to keep the gang going for the next few days. This event put everyone on their mettle. Time was beginning to run out for Abu Jildeh. More encouraging news started to trickle in that some of the gangsters were deserting and leaving the area. A second attempted raid on an outpost found the police well prepared; the assailants were beaten off and one of them was wounded and captured. From him there came information which showed that if pressure was maintained, the end could not be far away. For Abu Jildeh was desperate for food, and was apparently hoping to break out from his home ground and move over into Transjordan, but was hesitating because he knew that as a 'Fellahin', a dweller on the fringes of urban life, he was unlikely to be welcome amongst the Bedouin.

A couple of weeks went by, and very little was heard of our prey except that it was known he was still in the area, stealing food as and when he could, and that his followers had dwindled away. Some said only he and Saleh Armeet remained. He had hesitated too long. He could have left the area and vanished into the blue of one of the surrounding Arab countries where he might even now be living out a ripe old age. But, as the final scene of his life was to suggest, Abu Jildeh was a showman, and he would no doubt have found that obscurity was anathema to him. Anyway the delay was fatal.

The end came suddenly, though not without a final bit of drama. A firm report arrived that Abu Jildeh and Saleh Armeet were hiding in a cave. Against this possibility someone (probably prompted by Abdin Bey) had thoughtfully interned two of Abu Jildeh's relatives and kept them ready to play their reluctant part. So now, a British offi·cer with a police party plus relatives hurried to the scene, and the cave was surrounded. The officer called for surrender, but was met by a volley of rifle fire. It was said later that he nearly had his legs blown off. I don't know, as I wasn't there. The relatives were then placed in position in the cave mouth, and, whether or not as a result of their blandishments, out came Abu Jildeh and Saleh Armeet, festooned with full police bandoliers and carrying police rifles.

The issue was inevitable and never in any doubt for either of them, and Abu Jildeh himself knew it; and from the time of his capture until the final scene he uttered barely a word. But there was obviously one thing preying on his mind and with the consent of the prison authorities a last wish was granted. Two women arrived with a parcel of clothes for him. He dressed himself in his new finery and, standing up with quiet pride, said that he would now die properly.

22

A Devious Affair

There is, fortunately, a code of conduct that governs the behaviour of British policemen. Some of that code is prescribed by law, and some is not; but British society is jealous of its rights, and any meddling with the status quo by the police or by their enemies can be relied upon to produce bitter resistance. Sometimes, rarely but often enough, the police themselves break faith with the code by which they live and work.

I remember at least one incident involving a flagrant breach of the rules. It occurred in Jerusalem and I was an active, if reluctant, participant. If any one emerged with credit it was without any doubt the villain himself. Had RGB known there would have been a mighty explosion, for the 'Police Idea' as he called it was engraved on his philosophical stone. 'Directions prescribed by society are not to be broken. I may not like some of them, but I have to obey them, and so therefore have you.'

I was doing a spell of duty at police headquarters and was attached to a new section of CID then being built up. This was called, believe it or not, the Modus Operandi Bureau. The system was familiar to most police forces in Europe, but it is doubtful if anybody in the Middle East knew anything about it. RGB, despite doubts expressed by his officers, was determined to give it a trial.

Now the Modus system depends entirely on the mind and outlook of the villain. Experience in Europe had shown that a person who had once successfully carried out a particular 'job', would almost certainly repeat the procedure, using the same tactics. Critics said that the local Palestinian criminal was essentially an opportunist who conformed to no set pattern, though they (the critics) remained open-minded about some of the big international operators who not infrequently descended on Palestine.

So here, propelled by RGB, was the Palestine Police force with its own elaborate card index system into which were fed details from all over the country of every crime involving dishonesty. And oddly enough it was already clear that just now and again a criminal did in fact use approximately the same method, but results were still a bit nebulous, and the whole system was very much in the experimental stage. And there was I planted at a desk surrounded by a card index system which grew constantly, very much aware of the expectation of RGB that the thing had to be made to work.

And then something began to happen. This process eventually extended into some three or four months. It really did look as though somebody was at work in Jerusalem itself, and that very similar methods were always employed. I conveyed the news to RGB through the appropriate channels. The Chief almost immediately, paid a personal visit to my rudimentary bureau.

'I hear that the new baby is beginning to walk. Show me what you've got.' And then after some ten minutes and a few crisp questions, 'I don't like ..... you will now alter your own modus, and will do it this way. You will find it better. However I think that you may be on to something. You will arrange for me to be kept informed'.

And the cause of all this interest? The citizens of Jerusalem had started to be plagued by a series of burglaries. These were all confined to houses occupied by well-to-do Jews and a few 'comfortable' Europeans. They all occurred between the hours of three and four-thirty in the morning (the Palestinian dawn comes very early) and entry was normally gained – so far as could be conjectured – through an upstairs window that had been left ajar; for it was the middle of the hot Palestinian summer, and as it was many years before the advent of air-conditioning, few people were able to sleep behind closed windows. Rugs, tapestries and *objet d'art* were, in the main, the items favoured by the burglar who had evidently fashioned his own ladder – presumably a collapsible one – in order to reach the required window. (This in the end turned out to be a correct guess). Once inside the house, usually a bedroom, he would pass downstairs, unlock a door leading outside, and then collect whatever he fancied. The whole operation in each case was clearly very carefully planned, and designed to take a minimum of time. There was even one instance of a servant who slept very close to the house being drugged, though how this was achieved forever remained a mystery. Of one thing there was no doubt at all: the burglar, whoever he was, moved more silently than a cat and – so far as could be ascertained – he always worked alone. It was clear, as time went on, that considerable pressure was being put upon Police Headquarters to end the burglar's career. Indeed it was known that RGB had been called to the office of the High Commissioner.

Special squads were employed to reinforce the usual night patrol system in the Katamon area during the appropriate hours, for it was here that most of the burglaries had occurred. But although there were many arrests of persons found wandering around without being able to satisfy a patrol, there wasn't a sign of any of the stolen property. Moreover it began to look very much as though the Master Criminal (for in such esteem was he held that his title was widely acknowledged) must have had inside information of police dispositions. On at least two occasions 'jobs' were carried out virtually under the noses of police patrols. How, we asked ourselves, were the stolen items carried out of the area without being spotted by us, the police?

A favourite haunt of mine, and of my particular friend Bill Galvin, was Jerusalem's Vienna Cafe. It was also used a good deal by Abdin Bey, under whom I had served for a short spell.

'Good evening, sir.' If he was in a good mood we would be invited to his table. Abdin had complete command of English, and was then, I believe, married to an English woman. He was a splendid raconteur, especially about life under the Turks, and we would listen to him spellbound. Gradually quite a bond developed between us.

It was Abdin who endured most of the pressure concerning the burglaries, not that any one would guess, for he was still regularly to be seen in the Vienna, and his uproarious bellows of laughter, usually whilst recounting some examples of Turkish skulduggery in the past, were still heard as frequently as ever, and responded to by his eager listeners. And from time to time Abdin would come to the Modus Bureau and pore over the index cards. On these occasions he said little, except now and again to ask me for an explanation. And then one day Abdin seemed quieter than usual, and appeared to have a far-away look in his eye.

Now I must divert for a moment. The next link in the chain of the story concerns my social life in Jerusalem. It was a friendship that Bill and I had formed with a European resident of Jerusalem that ensured the participation of all three of us in the events that were to follow. Bill and I were summoned one day to Abdin's office.

'This burglar', began Abdin in a confidential manner, 'you see I now know who he is; there are ways of discovering these things, given time; and I can even get messages to him, but of course he doesn't know they come from me – at least I hope not – otherwise the plan I have made will be no good.' And Abdin threw back his head and roared with laughter. He then became even more persuasively confidential.

'This plan, Mr Spicer wouldn't like it at all, if he knew. But he must not know, and very soon we shall be able to tell him that we have now caught the celebrated burglar Ali el Masri, and he will be very pleased provided he doesn't know how we did it. Indeed if he gets to know I shall get the sack and maybe even go to prison, and for you certainly there will be no promotion. You see for my plan I need you both. It is certain that if we try to catch El Masri by British methods we shall fail, and the burglaries will go on until he makes a mistake. I cannot be sure, but I think he may have an informant inside the police. And so, I must use Turkish methods, and that is why Mr Spicer would be very angry if he knew.' Bill and I looked at each other with some apprehension. What on earth was coming? It looked as though we were likely to be up to the neck in something not entirely kosher. 'Of course' went on Abdin, 'If the Turks were here it would all be very easy. We would steal some property from a house, plant it on El Masri, and then arrest him before he had time to get it away, and he would go to prison for a long time. But now, that kind of thing is too dangerous. We have not got any evidence to take him to court, and so we have to do some small things to get him there.' He turned to me.

'You are very friendly, I think, with Mr. Brown?' I nodded. Brown was a cheerful soul with a buccaneering mind which contrasted oddly with his undeniable status as an orientalist and an all-round scholar. He seemed to have no family entanglements, was evidently well off, and his hobby was collecting and keeping in his Jerusalem home just the kind of things that El Masri was wont to go for. I had got to know him through a family introduction and, with Bill, was frequently at his house. Brown was interested in the career of the burglar, and boasted that if his house was visited he – a very light sleeper – would hear, and would have no hesitation in using the revolver that he kept at night ready to hand.

Abdin's idea, in brief, was that I should approach Brown, and get his permission for his house to be burgled.

'We need to be only just a little Turkish', said Abdin. 'I shall arrange to have El Masri informed that Mr Brown's house is just the kind of place that he would like, which is quite true, but that it would be too dangerous to try to burgle it.'

'For a little while we shall continue to do this, saying what fine things Brown has been buying, and El Masri will start to get interested. And then one day we shall tell him that Brown will be away in Jaffa for one night, and that there will be nobody in the house. The only trouble is that El Masri will have to break his usual Modus, because of course Brown would not leave open an upstairs window if he had to be absent, and of course he would be making special arrangements with the police for patrols to watch the house. So, El Masri will have to make his entrance in some other way – possibly by forcing a window, which he has done very occasionally.' Abdin continued: 'When El Masri arrives we shall be there to greet him. But to make quite sure that he does not give us the slip, we shall need two more British policemen, and these I shall pick. I cannot use Arabs because you know something of our locals' – and he made a seesaw motion with his hand – 'somebody may talk, and this would be very dangerous.'

So this was it. There was of course no real option, for certainly all wanted to see the end of the burglaries, and it was for some of us a case of anything for a bit of excitement.

In due course Brown, being the sort of man he was, agreed with enthusiasm to having his house burgled, though of course he had no intention of going to Jaffa; he intended to be in at the kill. And so the stage was set; and about a month after the conversation with Abdin who, in the meantime through his own channels, had been in touch with El Masri, a night was arranged. Brown, whose theatricals over the whole thing are worthy of a separate story, was nominally to be in Jaffa, whilst Abdin, Bill and I and the two others were to get ourselves as unobtrusively as we could into Brown's house where all – including Brown – would be tactically posted by Abdin himself.

All that would then be needed was for El Masri to 'play ball' and join the party whenever he felt inclined.

The night was pitch dark, for El Masri's modus showed that he avoided moonlight like the plague. Brown's only servant had been given a brief holiday, and had departed on the bus for Nablus. Brown had made it rather patently obvious that he was going to Jaffa, and he had indeed set off in his car along the Jaffa road, returning just after dark and secreting his car somewhere in Jerusalem, making his way home on foot. And so, after dark, each conspirator smuggled himself into the house, all prepared for the long, tedious wait that had to be expected. And long and tiresome it certainly was. Around midnight some snores started to come from Abdin's corner. He had decided that under the circumstances a break-in would be more likely to occur on the ground floor. Accordingly he, Bill, Brown and I were arranged along the three sides of a passage that enclosed the two downstairs rooms where most of the expensive items were kept. The two remaining members of the party were posted upstairs, just in case.

From 2 am onwards tension began to grow. Certainly I felt it, and all sorts of questions began to grow in my mind. What would be the outcome of all this? Would Abdin's stage management really pay off? What were the mechanics of those extraordinary communications between Abdin and El Masri? The whole thing seemed really too much to hope for. What kind of man was El Masri? What did he look like? If indeed he fell for the plot and actually arrived would he submit easily, or would there be a scrap? I was distinctly nervous as I trained my ears to pick up the slightest noise from outside.

The night seemed endless. I must have looked at my watch a hundred times. The minutes seemed to crawl. What were the others doing? Had Brown drunk too much 'Scotch' to stay awake? Would El Masri really make his expected entry through the window near the back of the house screened by a tree? It was here that Abdin lay in wait sitting on the floor. Or might it be through the window very close to me, and if so would the others get to me in time to lend a hand?

The hours went by: 4 am, surely something must happen soon. I began to feel not only tired but irritated. Then suddenly there was the tinkle of breaking glass, and something hard fell to the tiled floor of the passage between me and the next picket, Bill. So this was it. It was through Bill's window that El Masri was emerging. Or had he already come? But if so, why the silence? And surely El Masri must have been uncharacteristically clumsy to have broken a window and made all that noise. Was Bill alright? Some awful thought went through my mind. A long tense pause; not another sound until after some minutes there came a curious slithering noise along the passage, followed by more silence. Then a pin-point of light. Was El Masri really in the house? Suddenly electric light flooded the passage. 'Out-Turked, by Allah!' shouted Abdin, with which he burst into bellows of laughter. Held in his hand was a scrap of paper, and on it was written something in Arabic. Abdin, slithering on his portly stomach across the floor, and getting cut in the process on broken glass, read by the light of his torch. We stood there dumfounded, waiting for Abdin to recover. I found myself giggling at Brown's appearance, hair standing on end, and peering myopically through glasses that seemed somehow to have got upside down on his nose. Abdin's mood changed dramatically and he turned to Brown.

'Mr Brown, I am so very sorry, for I fear that you have already been burgled. I am very much afraid that if you look in your study you will find that your fine carpet is missing.'

El Masri's note, thrown through the window wrapped round a stone, showed that he had played the policeman at his own game, and that he had come and gone before any of the police party were in position. The modus system had fooled everybody. From a chatty letter that he sent later on to Abdin, it seemed that El Masri had used a skeleton key of his own manufacture to enter through a garden door, and thence into the house itself. He had occasionally used this method, he said, for particularly promising 'prospects'. Brown's house had for some time been on his list as a 'four star' prospect richly deserving of special treatment. El Masri, furthermore, always kept his prospects under surveillance through a series of helpers, and this went on for some while before the actual 'job' which he always carried out on his own. It appeared that none of his helpers except for two trusted lieutenants, with whom he shared the loot, knew El Masri or what he looked like. El Masri had indeed fallen for the bait of Brown's absence, but somehow, as zero hour approached, his intuition told him that something was wrong, for he had been a trifle mystified by Brown's antics, and he decided to break his usual habit by entering the house soon after dark. He had however only a very short time to operate, because the first of the police ambushing party arrived soon after he got into the house, and he had to make a quick get-away. However there was Brown's very fine carpet which should fetch an excellent price. He much regretted his inability to make a clean sweep of Brown's valuable collection; a collection that he had dearly coveted.

It was, in the proverb which Arab and Englishman alike understood, 'an ill wind which blew no good'; he had long kept the house next door in his sights and considered it overdue for a visit. He had, in the event, done very nicely. Indeed he had only just completed that particular job

Colonel R G Spicer, temporary Govenor of Rome, from a painting
by Clemento Tavuri, Ravello, Italy, 1944

RGB as Inspector General of Police, Palestine, 1932

Group of police recruits, Mount Scopus May 1932
Author is third from left

when, feeling somewhat guilty about Abdin and his party, the assembly of which he had witnessed from nearby, he wrote his note and flung it through the window of Brown's house, hoping that the party had not had too long to wait, and regretting his inability to be present.

Of course the question that everyone in police circles was asking was how did the burglar manage always to get clear away with his loot which was often fairly bulky. El Masri's letter to Abdin provided no answer. Indeed, there was no answer of any kind until eventually one of El Masri's coterie was arrested for another offence and boasted (as is often the way with criminals) about his association with the gang. El Masri himself had by then left Palestine. He said, when interrogated, that El Masri had used a series of hide-outs in the residential area of Jerusalem and had been in the habit of caching the stolen property which, at a suitable opportunity during the daylight hours, would be picked up and taken on donkey back to the Old City whence in due course they would be removed to Middle East cities outside Palestine. Of course, there were plenty of suitable dealers waiting to receive them. It had evidently been a lucrative game which El Masri had played in a highly professional manner. Brown accepted his loss very well, and was so taken with Abdin that he joined the Vienna Cafe gatherings and the pair became close friends. In many ways it was a case of 'like goes to like'. Abdin himself emerged from the business with a commendation!

After his discomfiture at the hands of El Masri, Abdin wondered with some trepidation about the consequence of his scheme. He need not have worried. About a couple of weeks after the night of the long and abortive ambush he had been sent for by RGB. After an anxious wait, while he prepared himself for whatever might happen, he was ushered into the presence and warmly congratulated upon his success in making life so difficult for the burglar that he (the burglar) had found it expedient to leave Palestine for good. As Abdin explained later in the Vienna, he stood there for a moment completely at a loss, until RGB produced a letter addressed to him, written in English and signed by El Masri. In it, the famous burglar praised the zeal of his police opponent and said that on this account, because the whole thing had become too dangerous to continue, he proposed to quit the Palestinian field of combat and try his luck elsewhere. Not one word was there about the devious plot to trap him, which of course had become clear to El Masri. Despite much suspicion, no inside informant was ever uncovered.

Perhaps it should be explained that there is a provision in law that makes it a criminal offence to encourage a person to commit a felony. And that of course is exactly what was done at the instigation of the police in this case. The law had been broken by the police themselves. How much was guessed by RGB nobody ever knew, for he was always sharper than friend or foe, and Abdin, whilst being congratulated, had detected a distinct twinkle in the Chief's eye. As Abdin put it later in the Vienna, 'For an Egyptian, El Masri [his name means The Egyptian] must have been a good fellow. Abdin was prejudiced against Egyptians. Had he not once been married to an Egyptian woman whom he learnt to dislike exceedingly?

Sports day at Mount Scopus, On left, Hon. Patrick Wingfield,
later Lord Powerscourt, On right, RHC 'Tackle' Talor

Author and wife Elaine soon after their marriage in 1941

The Palestine Police march again.
Old Comrades Association at annual Cenotaph parade

Revisiting Palestine, the author, third from left, 1974

23

A Dawn Patrol

Dawn would break in about half an hour.

It had been a long, cheerless and chilly wait out there among the sand dunes and the scrub, some three miles south of where the first habitations of Tel Aviv began in those days; and if the conditions out to sea were as thick as they seemed to be here along the coastline, then this was just the sort of occasion that the secret Jewish organisation would no doubt choose in order to try and land a boatload of immigrants.

Quotas for Jewish immigrants there certainly were, in conformity with the spirit of the Balfour Declaration. But these quotas varied from time to time over the years and depended, it seemed, very much on the amount of noise made in opposition by the Arabs, or the persuasiveness of Dr Weizmann on behalf of the Jews. It was indeed a perpetual tug-of-war.

But of course if you were Jewish, and particularly if you lived in Europe where even then, in 1934, there were unmistakeable signs that Germany was on the slippery slope to ethnic purity, legal niceties like immigration quotas were not going to stop the flood of refugees into 'Eretz Israel', the Promised Land. In Eastern Europe, millions waited for the next pogrom and prayed for salvation in the tiny country which the Spies of Moses first sighted sometime in the 13th century BC, centuries after their Semitic cousins the Arabs had populated it.

They got there as best they could, whether legally or illegally. The Turks had been replaced as masters of Palestine by the British, and it seemed reasonable to hope that living conditions for the Jews might now be made more tolerable. Certainly during the 1914-18 war, and particularly after the break-up of the Aaronsohn organisation which carried out remarkable feats of espionage for the allies, life for a Jew in Palestine had become highly dangerous under the unpredictable Turkish Governor, Djemal Pasha. By the end of the war and the advent of the Mandate, the Jewish population had shrunk from 85,000 to some 30,000. As one Jew said to me years later : 'Most of us would have got out there and then, if we had had somewhere to go. There was very little food allowed us, and we lived from day to day wondering what new repressive measures would be introduced. And you British didn't help us by starting up a Jewish labour force in Egypt'. (This, with the famous 'Mule Corps' under Vladimir Jabotinsky and the legendary Trumpeldor, gave splendid service to the Allies at Gallipoli.)

However, the Balfour Declaration, so far as one could tell, had set the door ajar for those who wished to go and live in 'The Promised Land'. So, if you decided that this was the place for you and your family, then it was not too difficult to get in touch with a Jewish organisation in Europe that would show you what to do – quota or no quota. You would soon be on your way in some filthy and ancient craft that leaked like a perforated tin-can. But for the hopeful victims of European intimidation – and later the survivors of the holocaust – such were but temporary miseries to be endured without complaint. For very soon you would be arriving where the multitude of the Exodus had sought their salvation three millennia before, in Eretz Israel.

But landing in the Promised Land was not quite so easy as that. The British were vigilant, and there were stories of boatloads of people being caught in the act of landing, and turned back again to Europe, or sent to internment camps – perhaps in Cyprus.

In the case I now describe, the journey had been bad, for the ship was on its last legs, and the trip had taken longer than anticipated. There had been illness among the children and insufficient medicaments were carried. But the motley human cargo had somehow weathered a storm which many thought would be the end for them. They neared the end of it all at last. A thick overcast night, and the unlit hulk edged as close inshore as its skipper dared. And all the while on his mind was the danger of interception by the British, though at this stage the police anti-immigration arrangements were nowhere near as efficient as they were to become later, when immigration along the entire Palestinian seaboard became a very hazardous operation.

Suddenly the vessel's ancient engines spluttered. Full stop. The shoreline was not yet visible through the murk, though in fact it was only a stone's throw away.

The skipper wondered if he would ever get those faltering engines going again; and just as importantly if they would get him back to Europe? Strict silence was observed. Men, women and children, all carrying their miserable bundles of possessions, were herded into eight 'liberty' boats, which forged slowly towards the sandy beach. A flicker of torchlight from the beach, and the boats moved towards it and grounded. They had reached their destination at last. But no noisy rejoicings yet; though many of the immigrants bowed down to kiss the shore of the Promised Land.

I had seen him around the Depot for some while, a large, craggy silent man who, to just a few close acquaintances, was known as 'Alec'. Clearly he was not interested in the younger inmates of the Depot, and preferred either his own company or that of a very small select circle of men of his own age and background. For he was much older than most of us then at Scopus, and had survived the First World War; on his chest he sported the ribbon of the Military Medal.

After demobilisation, following a period of joblessness, he had joined the Black and Tans in Ireland, and from there in due course he had gone to Palestine with the early British Gendarmerie. On its disbandment he had joined the Palestine Police.

He was to be my companion on the night when I was to be one of a special party that had been ordered to patrol a stretch of the coastal sand dunes in anticipation of a landing from the sea by a party of Jewish illegal immigrants.

It was never clear to any of us in the lower echelons why suddenly, out of the blue, these patrols – sporadic and irregular – were ordered at very short notice direct from Headquarters. There is no doubt but that the Jews were clam-like about their illegal immigration tactics, and ruthless in their own security methods. It is highly improbable that any of their number talked. However, as events were to show on this and other occasions, the information – wherever it came from – was accurate as to both time and place.

Our patrol consisted of some twenty men under a British Inspector. We assembled at the Jaffa police station and were paired off in twos – the plan being that each unit was to cover approximately half a mile of coastline. Behind the dunes, patrolling along a sandy track, there were to be two police tenders, the commanders of which would maintain contact with the static units.

As we got into position I remember thinking that in the

murky conditions it would be a miracle if we could see more than a few yards. My companion and I had never previously exchanged a word or even a nod. With the present situation precluding any communication over a whisper, I hoped that my presence might be tolerable even to the taciturn Alec.

Together we pushed our way into an area of scrub from which we could overlook the sea – if and when the mist lifted. We had been assigned to the end of the patrol chain, and nearest to Tel Aviv. Alec – so he told the Inspector – had experienced at least one previous patrol of this kind. He had brought with him a pair of night glasses, and with these he peered constantly into the darkness.

It was chilly, damp and dark, with all kinds of creatures biting at my legs. And, I seemed to be getting cramp. We had a long, silent wait, and then at last it was evident that dawn was not far away, for a grey-black blanket came down. Then it seemed that the mist was lifting. And then over to our right, apparently from the beach, there came a single speck of light, quickly extinguished. Alec's hand signalled, and together we crept through the scrub. Out of the haze, and just visible over to the right, came a procession of eight boats, over full of people. Eventually they grounded on the sand. Men, women and children and some babies in arms were being helped out of the boats, wading the last few feet onto the beach. Quickly they were marshalled together; the boats pushed off and vanished. A child cried; several people prostrated themselves on the sand; young children, half asleep, stumbled along with the others. They were heading through the scrub away to our right towards a track that led to Tel Aviv, the Jewish city, where they would be safe. I kept looking at Alec, for this surely was the moment to act. All he had to do was to blow his whistle, and one of the criss-crossing tenders would have been alerted. But Alec made no sign; he seemed to be far away. Suddenly I heard him mutter under his breath 'Poor bastards!'. Then, rounding on me, he uttered very quietly but with total meaning the one and only communication between us, either then or later. 'If you ever say a word about this, I'll cut your bloody throat'. And I never did, until now.

24

Riot in Jaffa Square

In October 1933, I was one of a 'Thin Blue Line' deployed across the road facing the main square in Jaffa (ancient Joppa whose boundaries adjoined those of present-day Tel Aviv, capital of Israel). We were to confront a very worked-up Arab mob variously estimated at between three and ten thousand.

On a visit to that same place many years after, indeed some sixty years after, I viewed the scene of that fearsome affair and found the square and its environs remarkably unchanged.

The Arab Nationalist Party had called for demonstrations against the British Government's Jewish immigration policy. The High Commissioner, on security grounds, had forbidden the demonstrations. Already, there had been a clash in Jerusalem, and though this had been severe enough, it was a mere skirmish by comparison with the events that were to occur two weeks later in Jaffa Square. The story has been told often enough, but is significant in at least one respect because, from its lessons, RGB caused a riot drill to be evolved. And the pattern of this spread later to many overseas police forces, where it was adapted to suit needs as they arose.

We were a line of seventy to eighty British, armed with pick helves and metal shields, and wearing steel helmets. In front was a 'screen' of twenty-odd dismounted Bedouin of the police camel corps from Beersheba. Behind us were some forty mounted men – British and Palestinian. According to the Plan, we would, if necessary, baton charge and sweep the crowd off the crossroads. At the blast of a whistle, the foot police would move off left and right, and the mounted would come through and finish the job....

It seemed simple enough. In practise the mob which had been gathering since early morning hit us first, sweeping aside the Bedouin screen. In the ensuing melée we all surged forward together with enormous zest, foot and mounted men and Bedouin all getting in each other's way, with at least two of the footmen getting knocked over by horses. My distant memory is of something like five seconds of icy silence immediately before the clash, followed by a hell of a tumult. There were three or four unsuccessful charges; then the massed melées. The horses were unable to charge on the cobble stones (we lost several that crashed all over the place). Stones came from everywhere and seemed to hit friend and foe alike. A young British recruit, Ward by name, was knocked unconscious by a rock flung from a roof. I recall vividly the sight of the gigantic 'Irish' Murray (Quarter Master at Scopus) standing over him roaring like a bull, till we formed a protective human shield. Murray was subsequently decorated. Then 'Jam' Faraday who led us – one arm hanging useless from an encounter with an Arab armed with an iron bar – shouting up to the balcony of the Government building. There stood the District Commissioner, Crosbie; the District Superintendent of Police, McConnell, and the OC Troops – Ulster Rifles – who were parked away somewhere out of sight.

'What about the order to fire?', shouted Faraday. He repeated the question twice, but there came not a sign of a response. All that happened was that the three on the balcony looked at one another. And then 'Alright, damn you', from Faraday, 'We must do it, we can't go on.' And out came the firing party. From Faraday there came the correct warning preliminaries, which were probably unheard above the noise and general mayhem. One of the firing party was laid low by a stone. Then the crash of a volley, and nothing seemed to happen. 'Bring them down, blast you!' from some of us, and then another volley. Several of the mob collapsed, followed by a general surge away from the square. Apart from some cleaning up operations, that was virtually the end of the operation. Many of our original line were casualties, and we lost at least two dead – both Palestinian mounted men – with two British policemen very seriously wounded by stabbing. (They both recovered eventually). Our pickets on the surrounding roof tops had been overwhelmed. As for myself, I had been feeling far from well even before leaving the Depot and being drafted down to Jaffa. I was very shortly after these events to lie for three months in a hospital bed with a bad dose of typhoid. In the first clash with the mob I was knocked over and lost my tin hat, and I spent the next few minutes with my head covered by my shield against the stones – so I wasn't able to play a very distinguished part in the proceedings. When we re-formed for the next bout, somebody threw me a helmet which was far too big and came down over my eyes, so once again I was rendered fairly harmless. I recall getting cut off down by the Mosque, and in order to get back to safety I had to behave like a half-crazed dervish, using the edge of my metal shield as a sort of flail. So ended 'The Battle of Jaffa Square'.

25

Another Side of RGB

We had a dramatic society of sorts up at Scopus, designed to entertain the good and the great of Jerusalem.

RGB and his wife Margaret often took part, the stage being another of the Chief's astonishing range of interests. I was commanded to take a part in one production, but towards opening night I was involved in a bad accident on the Hebron road. A police car carrying four of us went over the edge and crashed down into a deep wadi. I was the only serious casualty, with several broken ribs, and thus my stage career came to a premature end. Perhaps it was just as well. RGB looked at me more in pity than anger, and remarked 'We may yet make a policeman of you, Imray, but you will never be an actor.' How right he was.

I dared not respond by telling him that in my humble opinion he was not cut out for the stage either. I am no expert, but I thought he was fairly ponderous on stage. But Margaret was a different cup of tea. She was distinctly talented, and virtually held our stage shows together.

There was a memorable occasion when one of our Scopus 'characters', Peter Olive, dressed for his part as a curate and then missed his entry. He'd gone into the canteen for a drink to brace himself. Margaret, who shared the opening scene with him, improvised madly for a minute or two and finally said 'I can't go on'. Down came the curtain. I don't remember precisely how the matter was resolved on stage (still nursing my wounds I was appointed to a junior stage hand's role) but I do recall a shamefaced Olive appearing in his curate's garb, and RGB – sitting in the wings – putting his head in his hands and exploding with laughter.

Peter Olive was the subject of many a Scopus anecdote. On one occasion he was up before the OC Depot on a charge of 'eating a comrade's breakfast'. He (Olive) had a great deal to say in his own defence, but each time he began there came from the NCO in charge of the escort – 'Silence! Constable Olive'. Finally, the outraged Olive turned on the NCO and said 'Here, who's up on this charge – you or me?'

At another time, Olive was ejected from the Europe Cafe one evening. He was capable of making the most grotesque facial contortions. He'd been sitting quietly drinking on this occasion, but he kept making funny faces at the band, and finally reduced all the performers to such gales of laughter that they couldn't continue, and the manager threw him out. Sadly this comedian never prospered very much in his police career.

I have said that RGB was ubiquitous, and I believe that many policemen – British and Palestinian – who served under him, will have remembered with gratitude how he used to find time to visit the sick and injured in hospital. After my mishap on the Hebron road, for example, I was lying in hospital that evening very much the worse for wear, when round the corner of the screen came the Chief.

'You'll be alright my boy. You'd better be, we have some important fixtures coming up and we'll need a few decent innings from you, not to mention a wicket or two.' Somehow, I felt that I would be letting him and the side down if I did not make a quick recovery. He made us all feel needed.

It was at Scopus on the occasion of a big mounted sports day, that I witnessed a very brief encounter between RGB and the formidable Peake Pasha. I was one of the orderly-runners at the beck and call of the Chief, and Peake was out in the arena judging. RGB wrote a note and said to me 'Take this to Colonel Peake. Give him my compliments and say I'd be obliged by an answer'. Now Peake may or may not have been 'one of my Officers' as RGB was reputed to have insisted, but he was a pretty big shot in the Middle East at that time, as Commander of the Arab Legion, and with a remarkable record behind him. He also had a reputation of having a very choleric temper, and I trembled a bit as to what might happen. I did as I was bidden, however, and the great man received the Chief's note with ominous silence, sitting on a shooting stick. Eventually he scribbled something and handed it to me :

'Give this to Mr Spicer with my compliments'. I returned to RGB, handed him Peake's reply and scarpered quickly to the rear whilst he read it. I sensed that he wasn't amused.

26

CID

I was never much of an enthusiast for courses. But I did learn a great deal in the couple of weeks of a CID course at Scopus conducted by the gifted Corporal A E Harwich. The knowledge gained served me very well over my subsequent police career. We were given a smattering of forensic stuff, such as the theory of blood grouping and the test for human or animal blood; and we were taught a bit about the impact of various calibres of firearm bullets. We were also given an outline of the fingerprint classification system, and how to search for, identify and remove a fingerprint from the scene of crime. We were given instruction in footprints, and in general what to look for and how to investigate various types of crime.

There were also some useful lessons on mapping an area, and about how dogs – both patrol and tracker – should be used. I recall too (because we were both Police and Prisons) a grim talk about the mechanics of hanging. Indeed, we all had to attend one of those awful events.

As always at the end of a course we were treated to at least one dose of RGB's philosophy. On this occasion he spoke about the need, as one became more senior, to delegate.

'Delegation is an art that you must learn – yes learn. If you do it badly, you will regret it, but delegate you must, because you cannot do it all yourself. Now look at me – I command this force, but I've long forgotten how to investigate a burglary.' (He hadn't of course.) 'I need to have trained people to do that. Likewise I have to rely on professionals to give me the service I need for dogs, radio, workshops, transport, signals etc.' Then an implied warning that I, at any rate, never forgot.

'But, if a professional under my command lets me down, or can't do the job, he's out. Yes out. We cannot afford to delegate our very important work to bunglers, can we? Let there be no mistake....' Rarely did anyone make the mistake of doubting that RGB meant what he said.

Looking back, I realise that I was licked into shape almost entirely by the Head Constables and NCOs of the force. The technicalities were passed on by experts like Abdin and the Arab Inspectors. As for the officers, I am reminded that I only came to know reasonably well three of the most senior men who served under RGB – the Deputy Alan Saunders, A J Kingsley-Heath, and HP Rice, whom RGB imported from Kenya to run the CID.

27

Jabotinsky

Playing a somewhat furtive, but never-the-less highly influential part on the Palestinian stage at this time was one of the most charismatic of all the Jewish immigrants – Vladimir Jabotinsky.

Here was a highly cultured Zionist. A Zionist in a hurry, with literary and poetic leanings, and extremist views. And such was his political timetable, he would go to extreme lengths to achieve his objective, which was quite simply 'Palestine for the Jews – Now; and to hell with Palestinian protests'. He was indeed far more than just a plain Zionist – he was undoubtedly a Zealot with racist and nationalist overtones to his philosophy who became leader of the Revisionist group which was later to splinter into the two terrorist factions, the Stern Gang and Irgun Zwei Leumi.

All the same, some of those in high places who had come into contact with Jabotinsky regarded him as a 'gentleman' who despite his fanaticism would stop short at murder. Indeed Sir Ronald Storrs, the first Civil Governor of Jerusalem after Allenby's occupation, eulogised about him as 'a scholar and a gentleman'. Although he represented nothing but anxiety for us policemen in a troubled Palestine, we mostly had a grudging admiration for him, and I can't resist a few observations on his background.

Throughout my own time in Palestine, Jabotinsky operated under several pseudonyms and was regarded as an

enigmatic and thoroughly elusive figure. Our Special
Branch, such as it was in those days, wanted very much to
keep tabs on him as a potentially dangerous 'political', but
nobody seemed ever to know just what his movements
were or where he could be found. Certainly he spent much
of his time travelling abroad lobbying for the Zionist
cause, and was as much at home in America, London and
the European capitals as he was in Palestine. And nobody,
apparently, whose job it was to find him, even knew what
he looked like. Yet, following the Nabi Musa riots in 1920
(said by some to have been engineered by Haj Amin el
Husseini, while others believe that Jabotinsky's followers
deliberately provoked the Arabs), Jabotinsky was
sentenced to a long prison term. This however was quickly
quashed by a Court of Inquiry, convened largely at the
instigation of a formidable actor in Middle East affairs –
Colonel Richard Meinertzhagen. From 1917 Meinertzhagen
had been head of Allenby's Field Intelligence Staff, and
from being pro-Arab he became a prominent apologist for
the Zionists. In point of fact, he was sacked peremptorily
by Allenby in 1920 for his open espousal of the Jewish
cause. After their brief interview he told the Field
Marshal, 'You realise you would have to give your house-
keeper more notice'.

Thorn in our side Jabotinsky may have been, but police
and intelligence records on the man were sparse. We had a
few facts on the card index, but they were mostly public
knowledge anyway. Born in Odessa in 1880, Jabotinsky
had been deeply affected by Eastern European 'pogroms'
against the Jews, and in 1898 he commenced what was to
be an influential career in journalism. It was in 1903 that
he first espoused Zionism, following a meeting with
Theodor Hertzl, the Austrian journalist who was the
father figure of the Zionist cause. But moderation was
anathema to Jabotinsky, and he became increasingly
dissatisfied with delays and divided counsels. At the

outset of the First World War, believing that in Britain he had a potential ally, he persuaded the British military authorities in Cairo to recruit a mule-transport battalion for action with the British Army, and this was engaged at Gallipoli and elsewhere. Later there was to be a Jewish Legion which fought with valour under Allenby.

It was in Egypt at this time that Jabotinsky had met and enormously admired the redoubtable one-armed Jew Joseph Trumpledor. The latter was a highly decorated former Tzarist officer who commanded the famous Mule Corps at Gallipoli. After the Balfour Declaration of 1917, Jabotinsky visualised a mass immigration of Jews into Palestine, this being he believed the only means of saving the bulk of world Jewry. He shrugged off any suggestion that this would be at the expense of non-Jews living in Palestine already. They could easily be settled in neighbouring Arab countries, he argued. There seems little doubt that Jabotinsky and his Revisionists – and many orthodox Zionists as well – had messianic dreams of a new Jewish State on the lines of the ancient Solomonic Empire, embracing not only the Palestine of the Mandate, which ended in the south in the vicinity of Aqaba, but the whole of the Sinai desert as far as the Suez Canal, an extension well into Syria in the north, and a large slice of what was then called Trans-Jordan. Indeed the excision of this last territory from the area of the National Home, in order to provide a sop to old King Hussein of the Hejaz, was a blow to the Zionists, who had assumed after Balfour that both it and Palestine were included in the grand design. But Jabotinsky was undaunted; he was prepared to force Zionism through and to create in Palestine – if necessary by the sword – a revived Jewish Nation based on biblical Palestine, the undivided Israel which lasted for less than a hundred years under Kings David and Solomon.

Throughout his political career, Jabotinsky found himself at loggerheads with some of the' moderate' Zionists like Dr

Weizmann, Ben Gurion, A.D.Gordon and Berl Katznelson, who all felt that the cause could best be served by a more cautious approach than Jabotinsky's.

His wartime activities in Cairo in raising Jewish units to fight against the Turks, had resulted in some savage Turkish reprisals against Jews who had stayed in Palestine. Thus Jabotinsky was regarded by many as something of a menace.

Very early after the Allenby occupation, it became clear to Jabotinsky that he was not going to have things all his own way from the British, and that the new Jewish immigrants into Palestine needed protection from the indigenous Arabs, bands of whom would attack Jewish settlements. So, with or without the consent of the mandatory authority, Jabotinsky started to create what was later to become the Haganah, the Jewish Army, using as his nucleus men who had fought with the British in the war. It has been said that Jabotinsky was at heart a soldier. Certainly, however tough or questionable his methods may have been, he will surely go down in Jewish history as one of the great figures of the struggle for Eretz Israel. What, for instance, would the fledgling Israeli state have done without the Haganah? Which leads me to another aside.

Whilst sitting one day with a Jewish acquaintance in Zion Square's *Europe Cafe*, a smallish nondescript man wearing dark glasses and carrying a briefcase, seated himself at our table. My acquaintance introduced him as 'Dr. Zeev'. The pair of them chatted for a short time, I think in Hebrew, and then Zeev departed. I had taken very little note of him. A few weeks later, again with my acquaintance, it was 'Do you remember Dr. Zeev?' I said I did vaguely. 'That was Vladimir Jabotinsky.'

Of course I already knew a little about Jabotinsky, but it was at this stage that I started to take a deeper interest in this remarkable man. I have no idea of the identity of my casual Jewish acquaintance. For all I know he may well have developed into one of the 'terrorists' who later took up so much police time and energy. I couldn't now describe him. Our mutual bond was books, and I do recall his interest in the then recently published *Marlborough, His life and Times* by Winston Churchill. Jabotinsky's name, because he was a known Revisionist of top rank, became associated in the minds of many with the murder in Tel Aviv of Dr Chaim Arlosoroff, a moderate and highly respected Zionist. A Revisionist named Stavsky was arrested, tried, convicted and sentenced to death for the murder. As a Court Orderly, I had witnessed most of the trial. Later, the Court of Appeal quashed the conviction and Stavsky went free. That evening, Stavsky having just emerged from Jerusalem prison's ghastly condemned cells, danced on a table at the *Vienna Cafe*. Abdin Bey looked at him. 'I don't like that bastard', he growled, 'but I believe the Court of Appeal is right. I don't think he killed Arlosoroff, and neither do I believe that Jabotinsky had anything to do with it.'

Abdin was usually right.

Events were to prove that Stavsky did not in fact commit the murder. He – Stavsky – was to die later in a Jewish inter-factional gun battle, the Altalena incident, so called. Jabotinsky died in America in 1940, propounding Zionism to the end. He lies among the honoured dead on Mount Zion.

Such men and such events bring to mind one of the finest officers of the Palestine force, Geoffrey Morton. In February 1942, in the turmoil of war, he was responsible for the arrest of Jabotinsky's most infamous protégé Abraham Stern, the man whose name became synonymous with terrorism. Later, Morton became Deputy Commissioner in Nyasaland.

28

An Unforgettable American

I must pay passing tribute to an American who taught me much about life in general and Palestine in particular. His name was Edward C Blatchford.

Of my first meeting with him I was barely conscious. I was lying at the Jerusalem Government Hospital, gravely ill with typhoid. Gradually, as the mists began to clear, I became aware of a frequent bedside visitor – a tall craggy middle-aged man (in fact, he was then about sixty five), wearing a battered green ankle-length overcoat. I suppose he did sometimes remove this ancient garment, but in my memory he seemed to wear it constantly. He said that – as with the Arabs and their abba or cloak – it kept him warm in winter and cool in summer. Anyway there he was, dispensing cigarettes, literature and 'candies'. He'd stop at each bed, say a few words and on he'd go.

He must have watched me struggling to stay alive, because in due course when I was just about able to stand upright, having lost some five of my thirteen plus stone, I was whisked off to Blatchford's flat to convalesce. And there I remained for three or four weeks, splendidly fed and looked after by Blatchford's Arab henchman Eissa. I gathered later that all this had been arranged between Blatchford and Alan Saunders, RGB's deputy.

I had never, until my hospital encounter, met Blatchford, though certainly I had heard of him. Indeed nobody could remain long in Jerusalem without hearing something of him, for he radiated a very special kind of disinterested

and infectious friendliness. He had come to the Middle
East at the start of the Great War with the American Red
Cross and had fallen so much in love with the terrain and
its atmosphere, and with Jerusalem in particular, that
after the war he settled there, and lived for many years in
his extremely pleasant tapestry-hung flat close to the
King David Hotel.

Blatchford, a life-long bachelor, and clearly a man of
means, rarely spoke about himself, but every now and
then some item of his past life would emerge. I was once
regaled with a lively account of his activities on a Texan
cattle ranch where for a while in his early days he had
been a cowboy.

One of his few personal boasts was his connection
(through the Bliss family who did so much for Arab education in the Lebanon) with the great American University
of Beirut; and every now and then he would vanish from
Jerusalem and spend a few days in the city that was then
regarded as 'The Paris of the Middle East'. In very many
ways Blatchford was a true International.

He had a special affinity with the Arabs although – as he
admitted – the task of learning their language was beyond
him.

'I had a go once at their language, but it was no good, and
now I'm too old to learn, and if they want to know me they
have to speak American or French.'

Blatchford had made it his business to keep himself very
well informed of all the local Middle East problems as
they arose, and he had a considerable political sense. He
had watched the Turkish atrocities under Djemal Pasha,
and had been horrified at the Armenian massacres. And
it was Blatchford who first explained to me, with quiet
tact because I was British, the unhappy muddle that
HMG had got itself into as a result of its multiplicity of
wartime promises: first the MacMahon/Hussein
Agreement which led to the Arab Revolt under Feisal;

107

secondly, the 'secret', Sykes/Picot arrangement setting out post-war 'Spheres of Influence' for Britain and France, with a codicil giving Constantinople to the Tzar, which was 'blown' by the Bolsheviks when they came to power in 1917; and third, the Balfour Declaration by which Britain 'Viewed with favour a National Home for the Jews in Palestine', with the proviso that the rights and privileges of non-Jews should be preserved. Of course, the three proposals were mutually contradictory. Subsequent history speaks for itself. Blatchford, who first explained to me the precise nature of the diplomatic shambles, was not himself a designated career diplomat. But so profound was his local knowledge that for a number of years he had sat in the American Consulate General at Jerusalem. His role was undefined, but presumably he was the adviser on local affairs, and he became a much esteemed institution. Such was his standing, as I heard later on, that during the height of the Arab-Jewish troubles he was one of the few Westerners who could walk in safety through the Old City.

He was an ardent disciple of the past, and once told me he wished that he could have studied archeology. He knew his Bible thoroughly, and so applied his knowledge that he became the best guide you could find in Jerusalem.

It was from Blatchford that I first heard the very sensible suggestion that a newcomer should first and foremost, before doing anything else, go up to the top of the Mount of Olives and get his bearings. From here in those days (alas no longer on account of the mass of concrete buildings) one had a view eastwards of the Mountains of Moab with the Dead Sea at their foot, and of the Jordan running into it. To the West there is the old walled-city of Jerusalem, and beyond it the sprawling suburbs of New Jerusalem fanning out into the barren Judaean hills. Here, indeed, on the summit of Olives, the newcomer could visualise the past – the original Jebusite village of Jerusalem captured by David, which then lay on the slope

of what is called 'The Ophel' leading up to the great platform now known as el Haram esh-Sharif. Here – after
David's time – stood the Temple, now replaced on the
Dome of the Rock by the splendid Muslim Mosque. This
was conceived by the Caliph Omar ibn Khatib in AD 638,
but was not in fact built until fifty years later. Close by is
the smaller El Aqsar mosque. It was a continuing surprise
to Blatchford that not all of Jerusalem's western residents
could share his enormous interest – though very many
undoubtedly did. He was a splendid raconteur and could
make the history of the Bible Lands come alive with his
vivid and acute observations.

Local guides revered him, and perhaps they were a little
jealous of his encyclopaedic knowledge.

Blatchford was the soul of hospitality, and a stream of
visitors – some whose names were famous – would be
entertained at his flat. I forget most of them, but I do
recall on one occasion meeting Haj Amin el Husseini, the
Grand Mufti of Jerusalem. The conversation between him
and Blatchford was in French, though I believe that el
Husseini spoke English reasonably well. My memory is of
a smallish figure beautifully dressed in Arab clothes,
punctiliously polite, and somehow radiating all the char-
acteristics of a black panther. He was an inveterate enemy
of the British.

It was Blatchford who once voiced the thought that if the
extremist Husseinis and the moderate Nashishibis (the
other major Jerusalem Arab family) could have sunk their
differences and acted in concert, the Arab case would have
been more effectively presented. That may well have been
so, but the long-term result would almost certainly have
been the same, because if Haj Amin did in fact see himself
(as I feel sure he did) as the new Khalifa or saviour of the
Arabs, nothing would have deterred him from his aim of
ridding Palestine of the British as well as the Jews.

Another dominant character whom I first met at this time
(I was to get to know him much better later on in East

Africa) was John Cheese. He and Blatchford met at the start of the First World War. Cheese had been ordained into the Church of England, but held strong views of his own which were not entirely in concert with those of the Establishment. He liked to think of himself as an 'Independent'. Several years younger than Blatchford, small in stature and wearing a pointed beard, he seemed very mild until roused, when his eyes would flash, his chin would jut out, and he would demolish his opponent with a few words; but this was a side of his character that I saw only later on in our acquaintanceship.

Blatchford knew something of his story, and I learnt how Cheese had won through against a Turkish Provincial Governor who had imprisoned him for his importunities on behalf of a community of Armenians who were being hounded by their Ottoman rulers. Such was the force of Cheese's counter attack that not only was he released but the bulk of the Armenians' property was restored.

Cheese knew Abdin Bey, and there was much common ground between all three of them in Blatchford's flat. For me it was like listening to pages of history in some talking book. I am sure that Abdin, who undoubtedly had a network of listeners-in throughout the Jerusalem coffee shops, passed on to Blatchford a lot of the local gossip.

I have always had a passion for history, and I feel sure it was those encounters in Blatchford's flat that cemented my interest. Certainly it was about this time that I commenced to read Josephus. And I have never really ceased to devour the work of that Jewish soldier and politician who, at the age of nineteen in AD 56, started to gather information for his account of the Jewish Wars, was captured by the Romans in AD 70, and who remains to this day the chief contemporary witness of those tumultuous years.

It was, I think, in 1934 that the distinguished travel writer HV Morton visited Jerusalem.

He and Blatchford certainly met, and Morton's book *In the Steps of the Master* seems to me to have a Blatchford imprint on it. They certainly spent a good deal of time together during Morton's visit.

It was through Blatchford that I met several members of the American Consular Corps serving in Jerusalem. The Consul General was Eli Palmer, later to become a United States Senator. All of them, together with the charming Mrs Palmer, showered hospitality on me and some of my colleagues. The American 'image' became for me so strong that I always tried in later years to return to Americans some of the very considerable kindnesses I had received.

Few would think of the down-to-earth Blatchford as a mystic or visionary, yet two curious incidents remain in my memory.

The first of these occurred down in the Dead Sea area when Blatchford was conducting some American tourists. I was with them at his invitation. At a point later to become famous as Khirbet Qumran, near the junction of the Jordan with the Dead Sea, we were sitting on a mound eating a picnic lunch and surveying the incredible barrenness of our surroundings.

The year must have been 1934. The normally voluble Blatchford had gone very silent, and seemed to have something on his mind. Then in answer to a comment he said he felt we were 'sitting on history, and that one day.....'. It was in '47 that the Dead Sea Scrolls were discovered in cliff caves overlooking the place where we were sitting. And indeed it must have been that very same mound that was soon to be opened up as having been the headquarters of the ancient Dead Sea Community (probably the Essenes) whose Scroll Library had to be secreted in the caves on the approach of the Roman Tenth Legion. Later Blatchford told me he had experienced a curious presentiment about the place.

The second occasion produced quite a different reaction. Blatchford and I, with one other, were exploring the

Haram esh-Sharif where are situated the two Muslim Mosques. Blatchford suddenly became lyrical; we were standing, it seemed, on the site of the ancient Antonia fortress built by Herod. Here it was in 70 AD that Titus 'held the key to the Temple and to Jerusalem'. Blatchford gave us a blow-by-blow account of the entire action. It was as though he had been an eye-witness. His only comment later on was 'Re-incarnation? I wonder'. I believe that Blatchford had very little to do with the Jewish community. He had met and admired Dr Weizmann, the great Zionist leader, and he had been badly shocked by the murder at Tel Aviv of Dr Arlosoroff, whose life, as I have said, was devoted to rapprochement between Jews and Arabs. As for Arlosoroff himself, I met him once very briefly. It was on the beach at Tel Aviv. A young Jewish boy had got into difficulties in the sea and I helped to pull him out. Lying in the sand trying to get my breath back, I found a very fine looking, anxious face bending over me. Was I alright? It was Dr Arlosoroff.

However I don't recall ever having met any Jewish people in Blatchford's flat. I recall too that he normally remained somewhat grimly tight-lipped if asked about his early experiences in Turkish-occupied Syria. My mind goes back in gratitude to a very real friend and a splendid man.

29

Haj Amin el Husseini

None of the major actors in the drama of the Arab 'settlements' between the wars cut a more imposing – or in some senses a more Machiavellian – figure than Haj Amin El Husseini. He was a nationalist, a formidable politician and I fear a self-seeker. He was in many ways the inevitable counterpart of Jabotinsky and Weizmann; nature's immovable object confronted by the irresistible force of Zionism and international finance.

He was born in 1893, a member of one of the leading Jerusalem families, and studied at Al Azhar University in Cairo. His wartime record was obscure. It is said that he began hostilities as an officer in the Ottoman army and finished as a recruiting officer for the Emir Faisal's pro-Allied Arab army. Later, after the British occupation, he returned to Jerusalem and from then onwards became the effective leader of the Arab (and his own) cause, and a bitter opponent of Britain and the Jews.

For those who knew something of Haj Amin, the thought inevitably comes to mind – what might have happened had he not been on the scene during the years of the Mandate? Would the British administrative task have been lighter? Would the Arabs have presented such a totally solid and uncompromising front? Would the Jews have persuaded Whitehall to adopt a more liberal attitude towards Zionism and immigration? These are some of the many questions that must arise in the mind of the student of those times.

Haj Amin was no ordinary individual, and it is arguable that his force of personality lives after him in Arab circles even into the last decade of the 20th century. It is a little known fact, for example, that Yasser Arafat, leader of the Palestine Liberation Organization, is a Husseini, and thus a family connection bestrides the Arab cause in Palestine across more than three-score years.

It would clearly be implausible to suggest that without Haj Amin's activities the 1948 impasse, when Britain retreated from the Palestinian stage, would never have occurred. With or without Haj Amin as an opponent, the Jews – following the Balfour Declaration which effectively pushed the door ajar – were always certain eventually to produce a situation that would result in British withdrawal and the emergence of some form of Israeli state. Haj Amin, who had developed an implacable hatred for the British and the Mandate, was very much in evidence, and he must undoubtedly bear his share of responsibility for a very considerable loss of life – Arabs, Jews and British – during the years of the Mandate from 1920 to 1948. Running through much of the literature on the subject, there are constant references to the power that this man, at the head of the noble Husseini clan, then wielded. And this is supported by such confidences as can be extracted from Jerusalem Arabs old enough to remember those days. Yet in retrospect it may seem to those still interested that insufficient emphasis has so far been laid by historians on the role played by Haj Amin as a major cog in the Palestinian wheel. Those who had an opportunity even very briefly (as I did once in Blatchford's flat) to observe him at close quarters, must have been struck by the tremendous latent power, ferocity and ruthlessness that undoubtedly lay beneath the mild and sleek exterior of this slight figure. The epithet 'Black Panther' that was once accorded to him was apt. A revival of Arab Empire may have been in the minds of some educated Arabs since the middle of the 19th century. If so, Haj Amin would certainly have been determined to keep alive such a spirit. Like the Khalifa and Mahdi of the previous century, he may well have seen himself as a saviour of the Arab peoples. Historians may very well come to accept such a view.

Ruthless militancy was Haj Amin's stock in trade. The Jews and then the British, and finally no doubt the French, had to be eliminated from the Middle East by any available means. There could be no half measures and compromise of any kind was out of the question. But of course in his student days it was the Ottoman power that had to be broken. When Turkey joined the Austro-German side in war there followed a campaign on behalf of the British protégé Faisal ibn Hussein to further the Hashemite cause in the Hejaz.

After 1918, Haj Amin no doubt realised that with the imposition of the Balfour Declaration and the commencement of substantial Jewish immigration, things were not going his way. The Palestinians had to be roused. The Nabi Musa riots of 1920 were the first fruits of a new, undercover policy. Afterwards, at the instigation of the then British High Commissioner, Sir Herbert Samuel, Haj Amin was prosecuted for subversive activities and sentenced to a term of imprisonment. But the sentence was passed in absentia. Haj Amin had made himself scarce. He was quickly pardoned, however, and elevated to the office of Grand Mufti – a position of spiritual authority over Arab Muslims which rivalled that of the Sharif of the holy cities of Mecca and Medina. Thus was Haj Amin's personal prestige and power enormously increased.

The confused and broken promises of war had left the Arab world with a sense of having been betrayed by those who posed as their friends. Although Jewish immigration was the problem which all Arabs feared most, a fierce internal rivalry developed out of the post-war settlement. With the collapse of the Ottoman Turks, the star of the Hashemites (the family of the Sharif of Mecca) had risen. The Sharif himself, Hussein ibn Ali, of course remained as ruler of the Hejaz and guardian of the holy cities of Mecca and Medina. His family had been promised hegemony over all the Arab lands by Britain through the McMahon negotiations, except for a strip of land more or less identifiable as the Lebanon, while much doubt existed as to Palestine. Syria had been set aside by Britain as the domain of his third son Faisal (his first son, Ali, was tubercular and too sick for office); but the French, the mandatory power, would not countenance him and so he was made king of the newly created state of Iraq (Mesopotamia of old) by Britain, while the second son, Abdullah, was given the throne of Transjordan, carved from the deserts of Palestine, Syria and Najd (soon to become Saudi Arabia), as a buffer to prevent the new monarchies and Palestine from tearing each other apart.

Thus the Hashemites inherited two of the lands they coveted, but it was clear that the French would never allow them a toehold in Syria. And the Sharif's family had become too powerful for Haj Amin el Husseini's comfort.

Then in 1924 another factor came into play. The 'Desert King', Abdul Aziz ibn Abdurrahman, Ibn Saud, hereditary ruler of the whole of central Arabia and enemy of the Hashemites, let loose his fearsome Ikhwan warriors and took over the Hejaz and the holy cities. King Hussein was eliminated from the scene and sent into exile. The state of Saudi Arabia was recognised by the world.

As we have seen, in 1933 Faisal died in Europe and rumour circulated that he had been poisoned by the British. Much later on – in 1949 – Abdullah was assassinated in Jordan, and there were rumours that the Husseini clan was responsible, although by then Haj Amin himself was exiled in Syria.

It was at this juncture that Haj Amin – always just ahead of the gun – deemed it wiser to slip out of the country and continue his work of disaffection in neighbouring territories.

Despite the widely held notion of *Albion Perfide*, I sometimes think that Britain's armed forces have gone out of their way to engage in battle with one hand tied behind their back. As Liddell Hart says in his biography of TE Lawrence :

'The Englishman is not Machiavellian. He can never rid himself of moral scruples sufficiently to fill the part. Thus he is always and inevitably handicapped in an amoral competition, whether in duplicity, or blood and iron.'

Certainly the High Commission of General Sir Arthur Wauchope found itself in a hopeless and frustrated position in its attempt to govern even-handedly in the midst of so much duplicity and so many practitioners of the arts of skulduggery.

I always believed as a young and raw policeman in Palestine – and my observations were confirmed in territories where I served subsequently in more senior capacities – that our collection and use of intelligence was extremely poor. All too late, towards the end of Empire, when territory after territory was achieving its independence in the wake of considerable civil unrest, much of this failure was remedied by professional training. But in the days when, for better or worse, Britain's responsibilities as an imperial power were world wide, the Palestine administration like many others suffered irreparably from inadequate and misleading intelligence.

Haj Amin was able virtually to dictate the pace and tenor of events without a great deal of opposition. He was able to institute a programme for the purchase of every available piece of land and to insist that there should be no more land sales to Jews on pain of death. And because there were indeed many more land sales at prices that were very difficult to refuse, many death sentences were carried out by his agents without even the formality of a kangaroo court. He exercised total power over the Arab population. From the police point of view he was like a malevolent spider in the middle of a complex web. Very little went on in the Middle East and Palestine in particular that did not have the imprint of his influence.

Unlike us, he had a first class and highly effective system of intelligence gathering. Unfortunately for him however and for his plans, the Jews evolved their own equally single-minded information and intelligence service, and in the event it proved more effective than that of Haj Amin.

But of course it is necessary to state the other side of the el-Husseini story. He, like Jabotinsky and the notorious Jewish gangs, was a permanent thorn in our side. But he was acting patriotically for the salvation of his own country, facing a mandatory power which had turned from wartime alliance to the role of arbiter of his country's future; in point of fact, to the task of preparing his country for occupation by people whose homelessness and suffering, however tragic, was none of his business. By and large, the man who more than any was responsible for victory in Palestine, Field Marshal Lord Allenby, was sympathetic to the Arab cause and hotly opposed to the pro-Zionist lobby within the British Government.

Be that as it may, the very intransigence of Haj Amin, his refusal to compromise, became at last a cause of his undoing. It was impossible for the British administration (leaning over backwards to be fair and equitable), to deal with him. He would not permit any Arab to give evidence of deals with him. He would not even allow fellow Arabs to give evidence of the Arab viewpoint; or if he did relent, the evidence was carefully vetted by him personally. With a word from him the entire country could be paralysed by strike action and terrorism, banditry and guerrilla warfare.

At the outbreak of the Second World War, this unpredictable representative of a noble family was to be found at the side of the notorious pro-German Rashid Ali in Iraq. Eventually he fled to Germany and sought refuge with Hitler. Finally, he returned to Damascus where he backed another soldier of fortune, Fawzi ad-Din Kauwakji, in the anti-British campaign of the Arab irregulars, until 1948 and the British withdrawal from Palestine.

Ironically, he and his supporters successfully bamboozled the British and helped to bring about their withdrawal, and so left the real victory to the Jews. If ever a man allowed the trees to obscure his view of the wood it was the Grand Mufti Haj Amin el Husseini.

30

The List

My time in Palestine was coming to an end.

According to the 'grapevine', there was at HQ a list of men who in the opinion of RGB were suitable for promotion to officer rank. It seemed moreover that the names of those fortunate young men had already been submitted to the Colonial Office. At the time I joined the Force in 1932, no commission from the ranks (except for a special prearranged cadetship) had ever been granted. However during '34 a trickle of selectees disappeared from our midst. The first of these men who were thus gazetted within the force, John Fford, was later to command the police of two colonial territories.

Eventually it was my turn to discover that my name was on the list. I was astonished and never did find out why. I considered that I had in no way distinguished myself during my three years in the ranks (I had extended my original contract by one year) except to try to learn the trade, and to follow obediently the doctrines of RGB. But there it was. I was offered a cadetship in the Gold Coast Police, and of course I accepted. I believe I was the eighth commission to be given from the ranks of the Palestine Police.

My final breakfast at Scopus remains in my memory, absurdly. My neighbour at table looked at my plate and said 'That bit of bacon looks as though it has struggled up through the ranks, same as you'.

I was going to miss the wonderful camaraderie of life in the ranks. I was to go on to the Gold Coast and thence to Kenya, to a full and most satisfying life as a policeman in the Colonies in the last decade or so of Empire, before war came to change the world out of all recognition. But that is another story.

31

Retrospect

I have made five return journeys to the Holy Land, all in the years of my retirement. I well recall the first of those visits, and the emotions it evoked.

During the plane's final approach to Ben Gurion Airport, the myriad lights of Tel Aviv glittered below, indicating a vast expansion of that somewhat 'brassy' city. And there were other surprises in store.

A number of Jews were on the plane. Some were Sabras (Israeli-born) returning to their homeland. And here and there were to be seen first-timers whose experience of arriving in Eretz Israel was simply overwhelming. They tended to laugh and cry all at once with the emotion of it all. And their reaction was infectious. There seemed to be a 'heady' atmosphere, not only among disembarking passengers – whether Jews or Gentiles – but even in the airport building. For this was not so very long after the Six Day War of 1967, and the euphoria was still much in evidence. For me, if this arrival in Israel was not exactly a home-coming, it was something akin to it. A mood of exaltation persisted throughout the bus journey all the way up to Jerusalem, as I peered through the windows trying with no success at all to identify remembered landmarks. Where for instance were the Ramleh and the Sarafand of my youth? They were there alright, but absorbed unrecognisably within a conurbation of not very attractive half-finished buildings that have replaced the orange groves which once bordered the road between Jaffa and Ramleh.

In my time, Ramleh was an Arab town with a historical background all of its own. But since the Israeli action in 1948 the Arab population has totally disappeared, and the coffee shops – once such an enjoyable feature of local life – have gone too.

The bus crawled up through the Judœan Hills. Near Bab El Wad we came upon a burnt-out vehicle, retained in situ like many others as museum pieces, reminders of the battles of '48, when Israeli convoys strove to get through to beleaguered Jerusalem that was then so very close to starvation. I had read about how the Arab ambushes had been circumvented by the most prodigious effort when another road section, by-passing the ambushes, had been hacked secretly and at great speed through that rocky and hilly terrain. It was a 'last ditch' effort, and just in time to save Jerusalem from falling to the Arab Legion.

It was during this first bus trip that I became aware of the vast afforestation programme by which the Israelis have transformed the bare rocky hillsides of earlier days. And it was not just along this particular piece of terrain; the whole country – as I found later – had been virtually replanted with trees and shrubs of every kind. It was, for me, indicative of the good side of Israeli occupation of a land I had always known as essentially Arab. The Romans of course had started the process of denuding the land of its trees, and the Ottoman Turks, during their four hundred years' occupation, had continued the process until much of the country was eroded and desert-like. That was the picture that I retained over the years, and the Israeli afforestation struck me as especially commendable.

Anyway, here was Jerusalem at last, and it was good to see once again the characteristically ochre-coloured buildings.

My hotel was on the west of the Mount of Olives at its southern end, with that perennial trouble spot Silwan

Village sprawling away down below towards the Kedron Valley. I was up early that first morning, determined to walk before breakfast the length of the Olives ridge to Mount Scopus and back again. Alas I couldn't do it; I got bogged down amid a mass of concrete buildings.

Sadly, in this land of contrasting achievements and failings, the Israelis, have wrecked the Olives skyline. It had once been possible at a number of places to look down at the Dead Sea, and then – with a mere turn of the head – to look at Jerusalem's Old City down on the western side of the Olives Ridge. But no more.

However I spent my first morning obeying the precept learnt years before from Edward Blatchford. Using field glasses I peered from the Olives' eminence down at Jerusalem, trying to get myself orientated and to pin-point well remembered places. I suppose it was inevitable, but I found myself hating the forest of television masts that everywhere despoiled the vision of the past.

What had happened to the Kedron and Hinnom Valleys, remembered as having been full of rubble and general decay? Nothing had happened; they had simply been tidied up, and the Israelis had even commenced to grow vegetables in the Kedron. It was clear moreover that a big archaeological project was under way at the south eastern corner of the city wall. I learnt indeed that most Israelis had become very much concerned with the remarkable history of the Land.

This was 1974, only a year after the war when the Israelis, through over confidence and on account of a serious flaw in their Intelligence arrangements, had very nearly come to grief at the hands of Egyptian and Syrian armies operating on two fronts. This near-miss had shocked the Israelis into an obsession with security, and every man, woman and child became security-conscious as a matter of life and death.

Indeed this matter of security hits one at every turn. Young men and women in uniform are everywhere in the modern Israel., and it is not long before one or more aircraft zoom overhead.

Every Israeli is a citizen/soldier, liable to call-up at immediate notice. An outlying chain of settlements is connected by a most excellent road network to certain centres from which mobile armoured units with full air support can move out with massive force upon any threatened area; and the country is of course so small that delay in joining action is minimal.

Along the land frontier with Jordan, right down to Eilat, opposite Aqaba, I was again reminded of this security aspect – a wire fence is intensively patrolled by armed mobile units.

Here, within the old city walls, I was at once struck by the absence of camels and donkeys that in earlier years one encountered in every alleyway. The Israelis had stopped all this. However the 'colour' of Old Jerusalem was still there, though I noted that the Arab mood was unmistakably altered. Even so, walking in the Old City and stopping at a coffee shop, I was questioned by the proprietor, as I had let slip the odd words of Arabic. Finding that I had been with the British police during the Mandate, he couldn't have been more hospitable, and up and down the alleyway I felt I was the hero of the hour, which surprised me. But outside the Damascus Gate a money-changer looked at me and growled 'You are British. I want nothing with the British. They hanged my father for having in his pocket a few revolver bullets.' This deflated me quite a lot.

One had always regarded the old city, full of its own very special colour and atmosphere, with its heterogeneous milling populace, to be a place of pungent smells and age-old decay. On my last visit, however, I was astonished to find in the Jewish Quarter a recently constructed boulevard with shops and boutiques that had a distinctly Bond Street flavour. But from here one again stepped into the centuries-old surrounds of squalor. Here, of course, is the 'Wailing Wall' (relic of the ancient western wall of the Temple.) In my time it was faced by a narrow alley-way barely broad enough for three or four people to walk abreast past the bowing, intoning ranks of the Orthodox. Since the 1967 war, the Israelis had created a vast courtyard by the simple expedient of demolishing a lot of hovels that probably belonged to non-Jewish people.

It was within the old city, on one of my return trips, that I had a very special experience which has stayed with me. At the St Ann's Convent, run by the Ladies of Zion, I joined some tourists who were being shown round by one of the ladies. All was normal until we arrived down below at the 'Pavement', and here our lady – in some remarkable fashion – appeared to be virtually transfigured. Her exposition continued almost dreamily, but she was no longer with us, and seemed for a little to be of the past, a living eye-witness of the scene when Jesus was there among his Roman tormentors – as told in the New Testament. Emerging at last I found that all in the party had been enormously impressed. Returning later, I talked with our lady guide. 'Yes', she said, 'it is this way sometimes, but not always. Strange things can happen in Jerusalem'.

It must have been during my first return trip that I became captivated by the atmosphere of Galilee. Here, I felt, it wasn't difficult to picture vividly the New Testament scene, but I had scarcely known Galilee during my police service. Dominating the area is Mount Tabor, 1900 feet high. One can get to the top by taxi or minibus, but we climbed, when I paid my one and only visit, and it was a hard struggle. However the view from the top is breath-taking, and the hospitality of the Franciscans who live up there is splendid. Tabor played its part in Old Testament history, and much later on was allegedly the

126

scene of the Transfiguration of Christ.

On a lighter note, crossing the Sea of Galilee to visit the Ein Gev Kibbutz which, until 1967, had suffered so badly from Syrian guns posted on the Golan Heights, a storm blew up accompanied by rain of a remarkable intensity. Somehow I had managed to find shelter, but a large party of totally soaked American pilgrims were being led by their pastor in singing 'For those in peril on the sea' – not that there was any peril. And then an irreverent touch from one of the pilgrims: 'Hi reverend, can't you walk on the water and calm things down a bit'.

In upper Galilee I was impressed by the remarkable Israeli effort in draining the Huleh Swamp, as it remained during the Mandate, and converting the whole area into one vast garden for fruit and vegetables, and the cultivation of crops of many kinds. It also included ponds for the propagation of fish. This must have been a mammoth project, and indeed throughout Israel agriculture has clearly received top priority.

No tour of Galilee is complete without a visit to Caesarea, the city built by Herod the Great on the ruins of the ancient Phoenician 'Statos Tower'. It became during the Roman occupation the Provincial Headquarters, the seat of the Procurator. Although there is today not a great deal left of what must once – according to the historians – have been a splendid city, one can see a remarkably well preserved Roman theatre, and the remains of a giant aqueduct. Sea-bathing at Caesarea is excellent, and as you turn a corner, there is a notice saying, 'THIS WAY TO THE GOLF COURSE', the only one in Israel I believe. Well, that was the case when I was last there.

Then the Golan Heights. This is a large tract of country that dominates northern Galilee. Until the '67 War, when the Israelis occupied it – they have done so ever since – it was Syrian territory. It was from these heights that Syrian guns would shell the Kibbutzim, and the villages around the Sea of Galilee. It is splendid tank country, and well worth a visit for all that, if only to enable one to appreciate the Israeli fears about security should the occupied territory be returned to Syria.

On another visit I spent some time on the so-called West Bank. During the Mandate the name had never been heard of; that particular area of Judæa and Samaria to the west of the Jordan was simply regarded as an integral part of Palestine. Historically of course it is Arab-occupied territory, and only came to be called 'West Bank' after 1948, when the still-born UN Partition Plan was contemplated. After the '67 War, the Israelis occupied it and started building Jewish settlements. This has been going on ever since, and is the cause of much Arab heart-burning and Israeli heart-searching. I never served in this area and have only twice subsequently been through it. I find it desolate and not very interesting, apart from the few remnants of the Samaritan people and the tradition of the Pentateuch.

Since 1948 , there has been for Jews anywhere and every-where a wide-open door into Israel. This has resulted in two massive influxes of immigrants. One of these, soon after 1948, involved the Sephardic Jews from the north African littoral, the Yemen and elsewhere. The second wave has been the vast influx of Russian Jews, which is still going on. The problem of the Sephardim was accepted and dealt with years ago, and most of these people were successfully integrated. But now there is the problem of this new intake, and it is to the West Bank that many have been directed, though re-settlement has certainly not been confined to this area alone.

Only once have I been to Beersheba, and that was on my last trip. I had expected a fairly sizeable 'village' that had no doubt grown out of the original Bedouin-occupied oasis. I believe that during the Mandate this was to a large extent the case. But I was to find, surprisingly, a fairly sizeable town, and once again, large numbers of presentable-looking small houses that have been thrown up to accommodate considerable numbers of the newly arrived Russian Jews.

This whole area – Beersheba across to Gaza on the coast – is important to students of military history. In World War One the Turks and Germans under the charismatic General Kress von Kressenstein held this line against the British advance up from Sinai. Following two defeats suffered by his predecessor in front of Gaza, the new British commander, General Allenby, finally broke through at Beersheba and rolled up the Turkish line. In the Beersheba area, incidentally, they say 'it never rains', but on the night before my visit there had been a cloudburst, and there were sheets of water everywhere for miles around, producing near Beersheba itself a traffic jam that would not have disgraced London's Oxford Circus.

The 'Gaza Strip' was always Arab-inhabited. As with the 'West Bank' it was – under the Mandate – a part of undivided Palestine. Before 1918, though nominally part of the Ottoman Sanjak of Jerusalem, the Gaza area had in fact been regarded by Egypt (though not by Turkey) as belonging to Egyptian Sinai; and at the beginning of the '48 war, after the British withdrawal, the Egyptians had occupied it.

Since the 1967 war, the Gaza Strip has been re-occupied by Israel, and according to some demographers it is the most densely populated territory in the world. It is all Arab, the people being former Palestinians, and they are – to a very large extent – accommodated in a series of camps not far removed from the notorious concentration camps of the Boer War. It was on my last visit, by reason of the close relations that existed between our very experienced party leader (Terry Shand, an ex-Palestine Policeman) and the local representative of the United Nations, that we were allowed into two of those camps.

We were all horrified. The conditions under which these unfortunate people live is indescribable. Everywhere, conditions are insanitary and squalid. If ever there was an explanation for Palestinian intransigence, it is surely to be found here. Perhaps they do throw stones. If I were a Palestinian living in those camps, I too would throw stones, and anything else that came to hand.

It is regrettable that a great and resurgent people like the Israelis, who themselves have suffered so much at the hands of 'superior' nationalities, and whose expertise in virtually everything is so conspicuous, can countenance this offence against humanity.

In the garden of West Jerusalem's *Holyland Hotel* there is a very excellent model – some twenty yards square – of Herod's Jerusalem. No student of biblical history can afford to miss it. This model is fascinating to a degree, and I spent nearly two hours examining and considering the 'then and now' of history. In particular one can obtain from this model a clear picture of the alignment of the walls at the time of Christ, in relation to what we see today – the walls built for Suleiman the Magnificent during the Ottoman conquest between the years 1538- 42.

Only once have I been able to gain entry to Gethsemane. This is indeed a garden, and it is tended by the Franciscans who keep it beautifully. I know nothing about the growth and life-span of an olive tree, but when I was told that several of the apparently very ancient, gnarled-looking trees in the garden date back to the time of Jesus, I was quite prepared to believe it. When I lived in Jerusalem as a policeman, I did try unavailingly to gain access. All I could do was to look down at the garden from higher up the hill. My impression is that at that time the place was an untidy mess, in marked contrast to the beauty and order that one finds today.

The Garden Tomb lies just outside the present city wall

not far from the Damascus Gate. The traditional site of Calvary and the Tomb of Jesus is not far away, within the present wall alignment which – as I have already said – does not conform to that which existed at the time of the Crucifixion. All somewhat confusing.

The traditional site discovered according to legend in 360 AD by Queen Helena, Mother of Constantine, now has built over and around it the Church of the Holy Sepulchre. The rock-hewn Garden Tomb is in fact of the time of Jesus. It is sometimes known as 'Gordon's Calvary' because in the late 19th Century, General 'Chinese' Gordon considered that the configuration of the green hill (shaped like a skull) at the foot of which the tomb lies, was indeed 'The Place'. I personally am one of those who agree with his view; the whole scenario seems to me to conform with what we are told in the Gospel story.

For some six weeks during my time as a policeman in Palestine, I found myself seconded to a camel-riding party that patrolled the western Dead Sea littoral. I didn't enjoy the experience and cannot now recall what we were looking for; perhaps I never did know. In any case we didn't find it. I can only suppose that I was included in this party in order to 'toughen me up'. I was indeed suitably 'toughened'. Apart from a 'ride' at London Zoo, I had never been on a camel before, and my camel did not seem to like me much.

In the course of our journey around this totally desolate, evil-smelling area, we had passed and re-passed Masada, a vast circular mountain turned into a fortress by Herod the Great. Until then I hadn't known of its existence. However, we of the patrol were enlightened by one of our number who told the story in all its heroic detail: of the mass suicide in 73 AD of some 900 Jewish Zealots with their wives and children, rather than surrender to the besieging Roman Legion.

I have since read much about Masada. I have also been

three times to the summit and absorbed the atmosphere of this gory affair, and seen the available relics. This is one of Israel's show pieces for tourists, and they do it very well. There are some stupendous views from the summit. One can still see the remains of the vast earth-ramp built by the Romans for their final assault. They must have been somewhat shaken on arrival to find serried ranks of people all lying with their throats cut.

This whole terrain has been grim and desolate since history began. Nothing can change the backdrop of the grim Judaean cliffs sweeping down to this cleft, some 1300 feet below sea level, with the Mountains of Moab rising like a grey enclosing rampart on the eastern side. The Dead Sea still continues to smell abominably – probably on account of potash deposits – and now for much of its length there are hotels and bathing beaches where Israelis come down to play, covering themselves with mud packs which presumably they think will do them good. And overlording it all at the southern end is Masada.

Another characteristic piece of Jewish history has always intrigued me greatly – the saga of the Dead Sea Scrolls. Over the years I have read much about these remarkable relics of a by-gone age. There was that occasion when I had the privilege of a picnic with Edward Blatchford and his party in 1934, in sight of the caves of Kumran where the scrolls were discovered some thirteen years later.

Subsequently scrolls – or rather fragments of scrolls – were found in caves further afield throughout this desolate terrain. In the early stages of the finds there was difficulty in restraining the Bedouin from using them as fuel for their fires. However as soon as the tremendous value of the discovery was realized, Bedouin cupidity ensured that these priceless relics would find their way to the proper quarter. They are now housed at Jerusalem's University in a most fitting setting called 'The Shrine of The Book'.

One learns that the fascinating work of recovering yet more scrolls, piecing them together and deciphering them is still going on – despite many difficulties and sectarian jealousies. Perhaps these finds constitute one of the wonders of our age. They are believed to be in the main copies of the Books of the Old Testament in their original form. They take us back (with very few alterations) one thousand years earlier than the 'Massoretic' text with which we have for so long been familiar. And apart from the Old Testament itself, the scrolls so far recovered give us some detailed information about the way of life of the people who lived down in this Dead Sea area (an ascetic sect of Jews – probably the Essenes) from a date well before the turn of the old era – roughly between 150 BC and 75 AD.

It has been suggested that one of the reasons for delays in publishing the results of some of the finds, lies in apprehension that parts of the New Testament relating to the Life of Jesus may have to be re-appraised. After reading the book *Uncovering the Ancient World* by my friend Victor Winstone, however, I cannot resist the thought that there may be more to the matter than meets the eye. He relates in a chapter entitled 'The Promised Land' how an unfortunate Jewish antiques dealer by the name of Moses Wilhelm Shapira in the Jerusalem of 1878 bought from an Arab a number of pieces of 'blackened skin' or parchment which bore lettering closely resembling the famous Moab Stone. The latter stone tells in a Phoenician version of the ancient Canaanite language the story of 'Mesha, son of Chemosh, king of Moab...'. The parchment scrolls came from Dhiban, modern Moab. They were in the same tongue as the Moab stone, an early form of Hebrew, and in 1883 Shapira took them to the British Museum in London where the head of the Manuscript Room, Dr Christian Ginsburg declared them to be genuine text of the *Book of Deuteronomy*. The learned Ginsburg told *The Times* that the Museum intended to purchase them for the nation and that the Queen herself had promised a substantial contribution. A million pounds was mentioned; no small sum in 1883. But a famous French archaeologist, a well-known sceptic by the name of Clermont-Ganneau, arrived on the scene and declared the scrolls to be demonstrable forgeries. Poor Shapira's business was ruined and he shot himself. The 'fake Deuteronomy' was sold off at a London auction for ten pounds. When, some seventy years later, scrolls were found containing parts of *Genesis*, *Deuteronomy* and *Judges*, and the Chicago Institute of Physics applied the Carbon-dating test that was to prove them genuinely ancient, they were said to have been in the same lettering as Shapira's texts. I can only suppose that those texts now reside in some unsuspecting loft, dust and mildew covered, unrecognisable and forgotten.

During my earlier life as a policeman in Palestine – as it then was – one of our colleagues used to talk about the Latron Monastery, and of his relations with the Trappist monks who lived there. How they managed to communicate I've forgotten, or perhaps I never troubled to enquire. Anyway he was enthusiastic about Latron and the Trappists, and particularly so about the wine which the monks made and sold.

Until very recently I had never been to the monastery; I now learned with some surprise that this vast fortress-like place, approached up many steps, was only built in 1927. However Latron was a focal point during the 1948 War of Independence. It lies at the entrance to the Bab el Wad pass through the Judaean Hills, where some of the most savage convoy battles were fought.

I had much looked forward on my last trip to visiting the monastery, and after climbing the innumerable steps I was hoping for a glass of wine – or maybe two; but sadly there was to be no such hospitality.

At the entrance, when we finally made it, there were no

signs of life, and silence hung over everything. Eventually, our knowledgeable leader said 'I'll go and flush out someone', and with that he vanished into the interior, soon to emerge with the Father Superior, who looked as though he might have been interrupted in the middle of prayers.

I was agog to see what would happen, as I always understood that Trappists were under a life-long vow of silence. However, out on the porch, the Father Superior though not exactly chatty answered questions put to him and was affable; indeed I found his demeanour highly impressive, though alas the matter of a glass of wine didn't crop up, and I hardly liked to ask. It seems that conversation on the monastery porch didn't count in the overall ban on talk; or perhaps the Father Superior had a special dispensation.

I returned also to Banias, biblical Dan, which is supposed to mark the northernmost limit of David's Israel. 'From Dan to Beersheba, as in the Bible', Lloyd George told an MP who wanted to know just what comprised Palestine proper.

This is ancient Caesarea Philippi. I have left until last my impressions of this place on the north eastern tip of Israel, close to the Golan Heights, because I have found it the most beautiful in the entire country. There is greenery, there are rocks, there is water and there are waterfalls; and only just over the brow of the hill there is the ancient Crusader fortress – the vast 'Nimrod'. In Spring the whole hillside is a great carpet of wild flowers.

There is a huge rock-face with a cave within which – they tell us – once lived the god Pan. And the backcloth to all this splendour is the massive snow-covered 9000 feet high Mount Hermon.

32

Final reflections

I suppose Dan marks an appropriate end to my travels in the land that I still think of as Palestine, despite all its changes and its new identity. I recall that on one of my journeys I took with me as reading material a copy of Sir Hugh Foot's excellent book on the Kenya Police Force in which I spent my later years. It was called *A Start in Freedom*. To this day I read with approval Sir Hugh's observations on my first chief, Roy Spicer. To me he will always be 'RGB' and for me Palestine/Israel will always be associated with the modern and effective policing methods which he introduced. After his retirement from Palestine in 1938 he became Chief Constable of the Isle of Wight where he served until 1945. He then rejoined the army with the rank of Captain and was promoted to full Colonel within eight months. In 1945, with the collapse of Italy, he served briefly as military governor of Rome. Seldom can the King's Police Medal awarded to RGB have been better deserved. Towards the end of his relatively short life – he died at the age of 57 – he was awarded the CBE. But the splendid MC (with a recommendation for the VC) of the First World War was assuredly the honour most valiantly won and doubtless most prized by him. I never did find out where, if at all, his sympathies strayed from the strict path of impartiality. His method was straight and to the point, and it was based not on abstruse theory but on practical reality. As Hugh Foot remarked in his book, he used to teach his men 'that everything must of course be done to prevent, forestall or head off disorder. But when everything possible has been done, every precaution taken and every warning given and still disorder came on, then was the time (so he used to urge us) to rejoice that we had a wonderful chance to show what we were worth'. I can almost hear his words to this day. 'In the alarm and confusion of impending riot or gang battle in the hills each one of us should say to himself, "Now is the time when all my training and experience can be put to the top test. Every step I take today will be just right, deliberate, restrained, well-timed, and quick and sure and decisive as well. This is my big day".'

There it is.

I have endeavoured to catch something of the atmosphere and the spirit of this tiny but immensely significant, ever pulsating country: something of the 'Then and Now' as I have personally experienced it, firstly as a young police-man, and then as a returning traveller.

'Whose side are you on?' The question is inevitable and repetitive, and for me unanswerable.

If I were Jewish, I would no doubt be looking back over the centuries of homelessness and anti-semitism to support my contention that this was not only the 'Promised Land' but also the 'Rightful Land', the place marked out for a dispossessed and homeless people to revive and call its own.

If I were a Palestinian Arab who had lost country and home, and seen countless thousands of his people either living in unspeakable conditions – as in the Gaza camps – or else reduced to being second class citizens in neighbouring Arab countries, in these circumstances I would feel a sense of bitter resentment and outrage.

Perhaps it is a coward's way out, but I can see both points of view with just about equal clarity. I can only hope most devoutly that the good men and women who have sheathed the swords of Israel and Islam in favour of a negotiated settlement, almost fifty years after the creation of the modern Israeli State, and more than sixty years after my first experience of the place, will be vindicated.

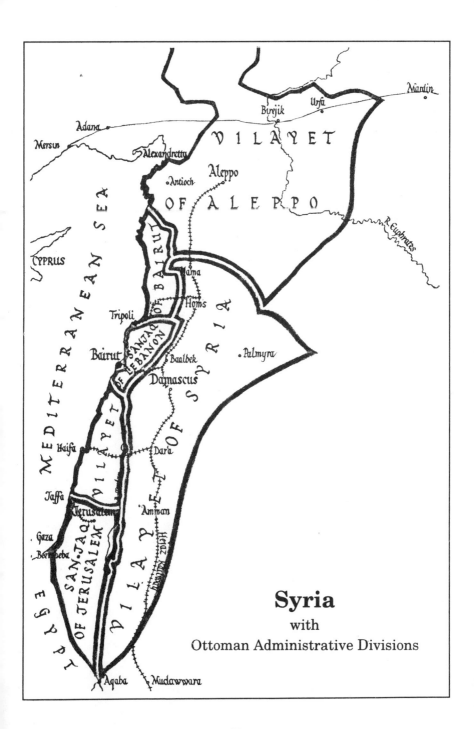

MANDIN

Birejik Urfa

Adana

Mersin

Alexandretta

Antioch   Aleppo

VILAYET

OF ALEPPO

R. Euphrates

CYPRUS

MEDITERRANEAN SEA

VILAYET OF BAIRUT

Hama

Tripoli   Homs

SANJAQ OF LEBANON

Bairut   Baalbek   Palmyra

VILAYET OF BAIRUT

Damascus

VILAYET OF SYRIA

Haifa   Dar'a

Jaffa

Jerusalem   'Amman

Gaza

Beersheba

SAN JAQ OF JERUSALEM

HEDJAZ RAILWAY

EGYPT

VILAYET OF SYRIA

Aqaba   Mudawwara

Syria

with

Ottoman Administrative Divisions

APPENDIX

Palestine/Israel

Accommodating Arab and Jew:
AN ESSAY ON THE POLITICS OF GOOD INTENTION

Contents

Visits back and forth to Palestine as it was, Israel as it became (as I write, the remnants of old Palestine are being restored to the Arab population in the so-called Gaza Strip and the Jericho region), have been accompanied by much reading and note making. I have gathered those notes together and have tried to present here a fair historical account of one of the oldest and most fascinating of human sagas.

NOMENCLATURE

The name Palestine almost certainly derives from Philistine (Pelishtim of the Hebrews), signifying people of Philistia, part of a well-knit and powerful confederation of tribes, the Purasati, from northern Syria, Asia Minor and the Levant, who from pre-Exodus times lived in the region now known as Israel, along the Mediterranean coastline. They are mentioned in the annals of Ramesses III (13th century BC) as having overwhelmed Syria and as an ever-present threat to Egypt. The Philistines, the Hyksos (a Semitic people who ruled in Egypt for about a hundred years from the 17th to the 16th century) and the so-called Sea Peoples came in succession to the the region, and between them caused widespread disruption up to and beyond the Hebrew monarchy.

POPULATION

Empires come and go. For Palestine, which forms a bridge – both laterally and vertically – between the ancient trade routes East to West and North to South, there have been very many occupations. Egyptians, Babylonians, Assyrians, Hebrews, Greeks, Macedonians, Seleucids, Ptolemies, Persians, Byzantines, Crusaders, Ottoman Turks, and the British; not to mention the Aliyah, the

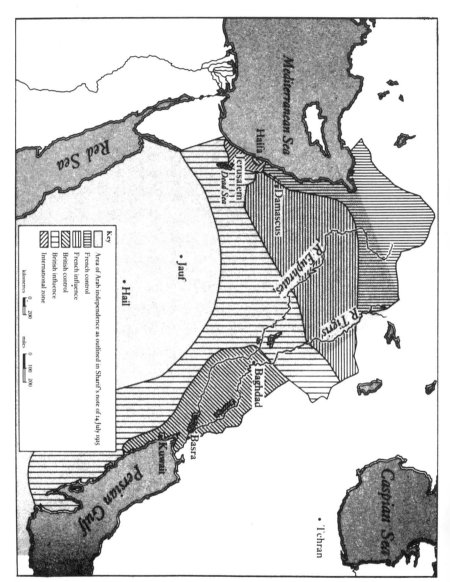

The division of Arab lands proposed by the Sykes-Picot agreement

Key

- Area of Arab independence as outlined in Sharif's note of 14 July 1915
- French control
- French influence
- British control
- British influence
- International zone

kilometres 0 — 200

miles 0 — 100 200

Mediterranean Sea

Haifa

Jerusalem
Dead Sea

Damascus

R. Euphrates

R. Tigris

Red Sea

· Jauf

· Hail

Baghdad

Basra

Kuwait

Persian Gulf

Caspian Sea

· Tehran

waves of Jewish immigrants of the 20th century who have claimed loudly, and with powerful support, that they are the legitimate inheritors of the Kingdom of David.

Inevitably, this ebb and flow produced a heterogeneous population that included many Jews and Christians in a predominantly Islamic (Arab) population. It is the descendants of these people who today are the true Palestinians; people of several ethnic and religious groups who were dispossessed in 1948 by the creation of the State of Israel. Most are, of course, Arabs in the loose sense of 'people of common language'.

THE GREAT DICHOTOMY

Jews and Arabs come from the same stock, known from the common basis of their languages as 'Semites'. The term, implying kinship with Shem the son of Noah, is one that was invented by a German scholar to describe racial groups whose speech is based on fixed consonants but with vowel signs of varying weight and value. The first such language was discovered in the 18th century in the shape of the cuneiform or wedge-shaped script on clay tablets and sculptured slabs of Babylon and its neighbour Elam. It was the tongue of the joint civilization of Sumer and Akkad (Accad of the Old Testament) which developed *pari passu* with that of Egypt, and in its original Semitic form is known as Akkadian.Various dialects developed out of it to become the everyday speech of Babylonians, Elamites, Assyrians, Syrians; indeed, for some two thousand years from about 2,500 BC to 500 BC it was the *lingua franca* of virtually the whole civilized world; even the Egyptians used it. As with all language it matured and evolved and it eventually became formalized as 'Aramaic', the popular version of which was known as 'Syriac', and Aramaic was the common ancestor of Arabic and Hebrew. It should be added that among the tribal peoples who lived in and around Sumer (roughly the southern part of present-day Iraq) in the third millennium BC and who contributed to the Semitic features of the earliest languages, were the 'Habiru'. It is now widely accepted among scholars, though disputed by some, that these people were the original Hebrews. Of course, Judaism, and the universal term 'Jew', came much later. It follows from the definition of the term 'Semitic' that it is no more indicative of a particular race than, say, the term Indo-European.

Certainly, those who are acquainted with both Arabic and Hebrew will notice certain fundamental similarities in the two languages.

On a controversial guess-note, let us go back into the mists of time and suggest that very early on, whilst succeeding waves of nomadic tribes came out of the desert lands into what the historians call the 'Fertile Crescent', there were inevitable disputes over areas of grazing and habitation,and over rival gods and cultures; as indeed there are today in parts of the world where tribal peoples are emerging into urban communities. The Habiru (spoken of in the Akkadian tablets) or Hebrews, would have clanned together, as would the Arabs.

GOD, JEWS AND ARABS

Tradition has it that Isaac, the son of Abraham by his first wife Sarah, is the founding father of the Jewish race; while Ishmael, the patriarch's son by Hagar, his Badu wife, is said to be the father of the Arabs. Since Abraham almost certainly left his home town of Ur a century or so before 2000 BC, all the basic traditions of the Jewish race must be dated to about that time. There are hurdles to be negotiated, however. The same traditions hold variously that Isaac and Ishmael were each selected for parental sacrifice to their demanding God, and that the intended victim was reprieved at the last moment, thus exemplifying their Lord's forgiveness and compassion and making possible the survival of the two main branches of Semitic culture. (For reasons which will, I hope, become apparent, I do not say 'Nationhood'). We know from the Egyptian records that even before Abraham in the third millennium BC, the region which became Palestine was an Egyptian province.

Nobody knows the way of it for certain. But I hope it is not stretching credulity too far to suggest that biblical Abraham gathered up tribes and tribal leaders on his way from Ur to Harran, from Harran to Canaan and Egypt, and back. We know from the Bible that at some stage after Abraham and his entourage departed from 'Ur of the Chaldees', they were told by Shaddai to go west to a country that he (Shaddai) would show them. So, led by Abraham, they did just that, and finally arrived in Canaan or Palestine. Abraham is said to have become a prosperous citizen of that place, centuries before Moses and the Israelites set out from Egypt. Incidentally, the use of the term 'Chaldees' gives us an interesting clue as to the date of the composition of the Old Testament. Chaldaea was the name given to Babylon by the new dynasty of Nabopolassar, father of Nebuchadnezzar II, in 625 BC, 1400 years after Abraham. The scribes of the Old Testament who referred to 'Ur of the Chaldees' were using the name that was in common use at the time of the Jewish Captivity in Babylon in the early part of the 6th century BC.

At any rate, Abraham's Hebrew descendants, armed eventually with the notion of a single God, the 'One-and-Only', and the assurance of 'milk and honey' in the 'Promised Land', established the religion and culture whose unadulterated survival in the face of three-thousand years of exile and alienation is nothing short of a miracle.

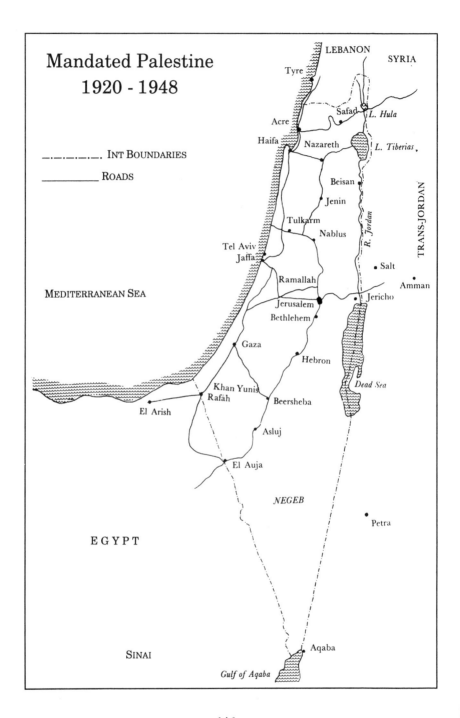

Mandated Palestine
1920 - 1948

_.._.._.._. INT BOUNDARIES

_____ ROADS

MEDITERRANEAN SEA

LEBANON
SYRIA

Tyre

Safad
L. Hula
Acre
Haifa
Nazareth
L. Tiberias

Beisan
Jenin

Tulkarm
Nablus

Tel Aviv
Jaffa

R. Jordan

TRANS-JORDAN

Ramallah
Salt
Amman
Jerusalem
Jericho
Bethlehem

Gaza
Hebron

Khan Yunis
Rafah
Beersheba
Dead Sea
El Arish

Asluj

El Auja

NEGEB

Petra

EGYPT

SINAI
Aqaba
Gulf of Aqaba

146

It is commonly claimed that the Jews were the first to adopt *Monotheism* under the guidance of Moses, which would have been something like a thousand years after Abraham, in about 1200 BC. But a persuasive case can be made for the proposition that Moses, who carried the cause of the Hebrew God with him out of Egypt into Sinai and there laid down His laws to His people, adapted it from a heretical pharaonic devotion to the single god Aten, the Sun Globe, which prevailed in the 14th century BC. The last of the kings of Egypt to foster the worship of the Aten was the youthful Tutankhamun, though he rejected the heresy before his death and reverted to traditional polytheism with a central sun-god, Amun. Certainly, Moses (the name is, of course, Egyptian) would have been alive within a hundred years of Tutankhamun's death in c1323 BC. Unfortunately, the Old Testament fails inexplicably to tell us who were the pharaohs of the Oppression or the Exodus so that we cannot date either event accurately from religious sources. But there is one clue as to the date of the Exodus. A stela or inscribed stone slab found in a temple at Thebes called the *Stela of Merneptah*, details a victorious campaign by that king. It contains the words:

> Canaan is despoiled and all its evil with it.
> Askelon is taken captive, Gezer is conquered.
> Yanoam is blotted out. The people of Israel is
> desolate, it has no offspring. Palestine has
> become a widow of Egypt.

It is dated precisely to 1229 BC, and marks the first known reference to the Israelites; and presumably refers to a time some years after the tribes came out of Sinai into Palestine.

Be that as it may, Israel spoke of the One God, whom it called Shaddai, later to be known as Yahweh or Jehovah. A long time afterwards the Arabs followed suit. Following the death of Muhammed the Prophet in AD. 632, they

147

proclaimed that there is 'No God but Allah', and that 'Muhammad is His Messenger'.

There are many reasons of course for what is now called anti-Semitism. Some is undoubtedly manufactured by racialists of one brand or another. Some, equally, is engendered by the Jews themselves; by their insistence on 'purity' and 'separateness'. Some Jews, for example, assert vehemently that there is only one relevant history of Palestine, the history given in the Pentateuch, the five 'Books of Moses' of the OT; that Eretz Israel (Palestine) belongs and always has belonged to the Jews. For them there is no argument. The case is closed, not by history but by the word of God. It is hard to argue against that proposition. But the picture is, as we see, nothing like so simple. No reasonable person can doubt, however, that there was already a population in the Promised Land before Abraham, and we know from the Jews' own record of events that a thousand years later Joshua and the tribes had to fight hard to find a lodgement. Interestingly, the term 'anti-Semitic' is seldom if ever used in connection with anti-Arab sentiments.

Orthodox Jews conduct their lives firstly in accordance with *The Torah* (The Law). Some Jews, on the other hand, regard the Torah as essentially a treatise in jurisprudence. Moses received the Laws direct from Shaddai/Yahweh somewhere in the shadow of Mount Sinai. Then there is the catalogue of dicta, warnings etc., attributed to the Prophets – and this embraces a substantial part of the Old Testament. The rest of *The Torah* is mainly composed of ancient history, verse and proverbs. The second main pillar of Judaism is *The Talmud* which embraces not only the Law and the Prophets, but also the *Mishna* which is a vast catalogue of interpretations of the said Law and the Prophets.

A remarkable degree of clannishness is inherent in Judaism that may be described as 'Separatism'. It is probably this aspect of Jewish religion that has been the root cause of so much anti-Semitic feeling since the days of the Roman occupation of the Holy Land and the dispersion of the Jews.

For Orthodox Jews, history and religion are one. For them there are two vital requirements. One is a retrospective loyalty to the first King of a United Israel – David. The second is an unqualified belief in the Messiah, who must appear at some unspecified stage, after which all wrongs will be righted and all will be well for world Jewry. It cannot be stressed too emphatically that the Messiah is not God or Jehovah (despite some Christian misconceptions), but a divinely-inspired emissary who shall be of the house and lineage of David.

It should be emphasized again that such are the beliefs of Orthodox Jews. It is likely that the vast majority of modern Jews (including the Sabras, those born in Israel) are, like the peoples of most other races and religions, too busy thinking about the problems of life in the modern world to pay too much regard to the demands of ancient history. Who was it made that profound observation, 'Happy is the land that has no history' ? A Roman perhaps, for I seem to remember it from school Latin exercises.

JEWS OF EAST AND WEST

There have been in the Diaspora (dispersion) two distinct categories of Jews: the Ashkenazim and the Sephardim. The former are of German and Russian origin; the latter are largely the descendants of Jews who once settled in Spain and were in general allowed freedom from persecution until the time of the Inquisition, but were then evicted and sought hospitality elsewhere. Most of them became poor relations in the territories along the north African littoral, and down the Red Sea coast into the Yemen. In

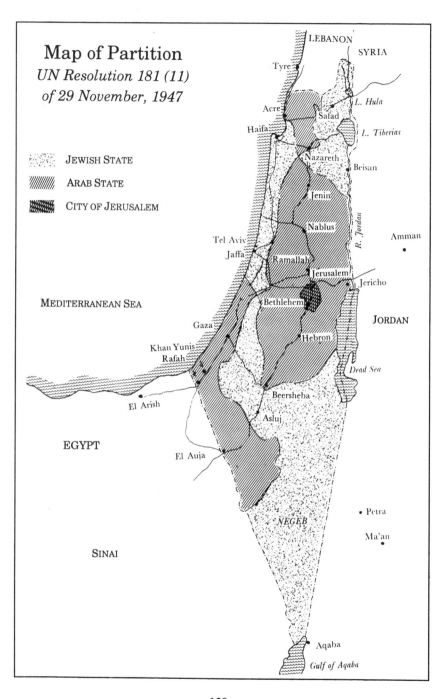

Map of Partition
UN Resolution 181 (11)
of 29 November, 1947

JEWISH STATE
ARAB STATE
CITY OF JERUSALEM

MEDITERRANEAN SEA

LEBANON
SYRIA
Tyre
Acre
L. Hula
Safad
Haifa
L. Tiberias
Nazareth
Beisan
Jenin
Nablus
R. Jordan
Tel Aviv
Amman
Jaffa
Ramallah
Jerusalem
Jericho
Bethlehem
JORDAN
Gaza
Hebron
Khan Yunis
Rafah
Dead Sea
El Arish
Beersheba
Asluj
EGYPT
El Auja
Petra
NEGEB
Ma'an
SINAI
Aqaba
Gulf of Aqaba

150

the modern Israel the two divisions of Jewry are slowly though relentlessly becoming merged, and maybe it is the Sabra (Israeli-born) who is becoming the archetype. Around the turn of the present century, there were several Aliyahs (waves of immigration) into Palestine, which was then of course still under the aegis of the Ottoman Turks. These early settlers had a hard time of it owing to the rigours of a barren land that relented only to an abundance of toil in draining malarial swamps, moving endless rocky boulders, and fertilising a soil that had known nothing but flood and sun-baking from time immemorial. This was bad enough, but resources were tight, the Turks unhelpful and often overtly hostile, and marauding Arabs a constant threat.

Somehow over the years, many of the difficulties were overcome by heroic effort; but life in the Ottoman Empire was never easy for any of its peoples, and Armenians and Kurds suffered just as much as Jews from an often despotic rule. But it goes without saying that Ottoman governors were not the only despots in the imperial world.

ZIONISM

This is a modern term dating from the middle of the last century, implying a return by Jews to the Promised Land. It has both religious and political connotations and the two are often confused. It is believed that King David was buried on Mount Zion in Jerusalem. But the idea of the Messiah making his charismatic appearance at Mount Zion has had its enthusiasts among Christians as well as Jews.

It was the Austrian lawyer Theodor Hertzl who turned a pious hope into a political movement. In 1896, he issued his famous statement *Der Judenstaat : Versuch einer modernen Loering der juedischen Frage* (The Jewish

State: Search for a modern solution to the Jewish Question) setting out the idea of a separate Jewish state as a homeland for all the displaced people of the Diaspora. From that statement developed the political philosophy of Zionism and Jewish nationalism. Within a few years of Hertzl's proclamation, a distinguished Scots theologian and scientist, Dr Torrance, established himself at Tiberias to await the return of the Israelites to Palestine. It would, he said, be the harbinger of the Second Coming of Christ. The First World War, unfortunately, spoilt his vigil.

It is the hope of very many Jews of the Diaspora to be able to make a pilgrimage to Mount Zion.

JEWISH CONTROL OF THE LAND

So far as can be understood from a study of history, there were only two periods when it could be said that the Jews were in total control of Palestine. The first was the brief time of Solomon (David's son and successor) whose empire embraced a very large stretch of territory including not only Palestine but also areas of what we now call Jordan, together with parts of modern Syria and Lebanon. But the Solomon regime lasted less than twenty years before the disruption of the monarchy and the establishment of the Divided Kingdoms of Judaea and Israel. David, to be sure, had ruled for some fifty years during which time a true Israel could be said to have existed, but his control was limited by the incursions of surrounding nations and tribes – notably the Philistines.

The second period of control appears to have been much later on, about 160 BC, following the revolt of the Maccabees against the Seleucid (post Alexandrian) rule of Antiochus Epiphanes. Before the Seleucid rulers, the Egyptian-governed province of Judaea had become a Syrian outpost. The Temple, sacked in about 330 BC, was re-dedicated in 161, and Jewish independence recognised in 129. This period of independence came to an end with civil war and the advent, in 65 BC, of Pompey. Judaea was officially declared a Roman province in the year 63 BC.

JEWISH SECTS

At the time of Christ, there were four distinctive sects among the Jews. The Sadducees were the aristocrats, the 'stiff-necked' priestly caste whose lives revolved around Temple worship. They did not believe in an after-life. When the Temple of Herod was destroyed by the Romans in AD 70 the Sadducees disappeared from history.

The Pharisees were the Scribes, the perpetual interpreters of the Law and the Prophets. They did believe in an after-life. Perhaps – at a stretch – one might equate them with the modern Orthodox Jews.

The Essenes were ultra-religious ascetics. They lived for the most part in desert regions, and seem to have gone out of history at about the same time as the Sadducees – perhaps annihilated by the Roman Tenth Legion which swept down the Jordan valley at that time. The Dead Sea Scrolls, first discovered in 1947 in caves at a place called Khirbet Kumran, were almost certainly from the library of the ruined Essene monastery that lies nearby at the foot of the Judaean cliffs facing the Dead Sea near the confluence with the Jordan.

The Zealots, with their 'hit men' the Sicarii, were the revolutionaries, pledged to drive out the Roman colonial power, and merciless towards collaborators. They were the precursors of many a subsequent Israeli 'hit squad'. They too disappeared at the sack of the Temple and the destruction of Jerusalem by the Romans in AD 70.

THE ARABS

As already stated, the Arabs of Palestine are the descendants of the diverse tribes who have lived in the region since very early times – tribes which are known to have been there before Abraham and his people, because it was they who brought Semitic speech to the land of Sumer and Akkad where the patriarch was born.

What in fact is an Arab? In all probability the term originally denoted the nomad of the Arabian desert. From the 7th Century AD, however, following the Flight of the Prophet from Mecca to his own city, Medina, the message of Islam became so powerful that Arabia and the Arab have become identified, misguidedly, with the Muslim religion, and with virtually the entire Fertile Crescent.

At the risk of appearing to patronize, I must make it clear that neither Iranians (Persians of old) nor Egyptians are Arabian, though both are in general devoutly Muslim. I must also make the obvious point that there are very many Christians among Arabs, Turks, Egyptians, Sudanese and other other predominantly Islamic peoples.

THE ARAB CONQUEST

The Prophet Muhammed (570/632 AD) produced a code which is as definitive to Muslims as is Mosaic Law to the Jews. That code, they affirm, was conveyed to the Prophet personally by Allah. The divine commands were collected eventually into the Koran and they made an enormous and almost immediate impact on the peoples of the Arabian peninsula. After the death of the Prophet, Arab armies carried the message and the green flag of Islam to every corner of the known world. Into central Asia in one direction, to the Mediterranean and beyond to Spain and France in another, to India and beyond to Indonesia in another, to north Africa and into the heart of that continent in yet another; the horse and camel borne carriers of the 'Word' of Allah proved irresistible. They were finally halted in France at the battle of Tours, in AD 712, but not before the most astonishing campaign of religious persuasion in all history had converted a large part of the old world to Islam.

It was a race of rather loose converts to the Islamic cause, the Moghuls (or Tartars), that brought about the destruction of the Arab Caliphates (the Prophet's successors), and by the most fearful campaigns of genocide ever waged, brought about the demise of whole nations from European Russia to China, leaving a power vacuum in their wake which others were ready to fill.

THE OTTOMAN TURKS

The Ottoman – or Osmanli – Turks, converted to Islam during the Arab conquests, were the best equipped to step in where the Khans and their Hordes had left so much chaos. Their influence on the march of subsequent events was to be profound, for their empire, which eventually embraced much of the Middle East, proved one of the most lasting in history, though tenuous at times. In fact, the empire lasted almost exactly 600 years from the 13th Century to the beginning of the 20th; twice as long as the Greek, Roman or British empires. It came to an abrupt end when it joined the wrong side in the 1914-18 war and was effectively dismembered by Britain and France. Turkish government is often referred to as the Sublime Porte, with reference to the Bab al Ali, the high ingate to the Sultan's Palace.

To this day, opinions differ widely about the conduct and nature of Ottoman rule. According to some historians, and indeed to some who personally experienced the Pashas and Walis, Mudirs and Kaimakams, their rule was harsh and cruel. Certainly by the end of the empire there were only some 30,000 Jews left living in Palestine. On the other hand the Arabs, by and large, did not fare so badly and many of all classes who lived under the Turks through many generations thought them an enlightened and comparatively benign imperial power. However, in the early days of World War I, the Turks took full advantage of French perfidy in leaving behind in Damascus lists of members of secret Arab societies. The result was a 'clean up' policy in which many leading Arabs were publicly executed while their families were subjected to shocking penalties.

The position of Palestine under the Turks was never entirely clear to the outside world. It was generally regarded as part of the Vilayat (Province) of Ash-Sham (Syria), forming a Sanjak (district) of that Province. However, under its correct title of Sanjak al-Quds (Jerusalem) it was ruled as a separate and self contained province.

It has been said that Zionism was a product of 19th century political philosophy. It is significant that an Arab 'awakening' occurred at around the same time. This may well have had two main causes: first, periodic Turkish excesses and ineffectiveness caused by the Porte's near bankruptcy and its consequent dependence on Britain, France and Germany who all fought over its prospective carcass; second, a hark-back to the 'heroics' of the past, viz the Arab Empire of the Caliphs. The classic *Arab Awakening* by George Antonius, a Christian Arab, gives a well-documented account of the dramatic shifts of thought and influence which accompanied these changes, while Lord Kinross, in his comprehensive *The Ottoman Centuries*, gives a pro-Turk but very well-informed account of the decline and fall of the Turkish empire.

SPHERES OF INFLUENCE

During the latter part of the last century, arising out of
the Treaty of Vienna and the formation of modern
Germany into a formidable and unified state, the Great
Powers engaged in what has been called 'The Scramble for
Africa'. And when that continent had been subdued and
suitably (or unsuitably) divided up, there came into being
the term 'Spheres of Influence'. For Britain at the term of
the century, the safeguarding of the route to India became
all important. The Persian Gulf, hitherto a 'British lake',
controlled by the Royal Navy without opposition, became a
vulnerable lifeline. Russia began to plan a railroad to the
Gulf and beyond, ultimately going via Kuwait and
Baghdad to the Mediterranean. Germany responded with
the Berlin-Baghdad rail scheme. Britain, terrified of
Tsarist aspirations, and increasingly afraid of Germany,
bought a lease on a piece of Kuwaiti land called Bandar
Shuwaikh, which was then the only realistic debouchure
for the German scheme. In 1882, Britain took control of
Suez by occupying Egypt and declaring what Lord Milner
called a 'Veiled Protectorate', despite the fact that it still
formed a part – although very distantly and loosely – of
the Ottoman Empire. This Protectorate really amounted
de facto to direct British rule through a Resident (on the
old Indian basis), with an Egyptian monarch sitting
precariously on the throne. In 1906, Britain and Russia,
frightened of each other's intentions, agreed to the division of Persia (Iran) into spheres of influence, the Tsar
having the top third of the country and Britain the Gulf
coastal region, with a neutral zone in the centre.

Britain and France were liable to get in each other's way
at this time, especially over Egypt, but Britain eventually
had the better of the argument and, indeed, stayed in

Egypt, from where it was able to keep an eye on much of the Middle East, until finally kicked out by President Nasser in the astonishing events of 1956.

PRO-ARAB OR PRO-JEW?

Very clearly there are two sides to this as any other matter. It has to be said that during my own time in Palestine, some sixty years ago, there was a prevailing bias among the British (from Whitehall downwards) and some Americans, in favour of the Arabs. I believe that there existed, and despite everything still does exist, a certain numinous kinship between Briton and Arab – they seem on the whole to get on well together, and there has for many years been something of what seasoned campaigners used to call the 'Turkish Delight' view of desert Arabia among Britons as a whole. Equally, it must be said that the big guns of politics and finance were always on the side of the Jews, and from the early days of the Zionist movement the Jews built up intelligence and propaganda systems that were second to none, even though they, like all other conventional institutions, were overwhelmed by the fascist machine in the 'thirties. For the Jews of the Diaspora the attraction of a homeland free from the future menace of persecution and pogrom was incentive enough to claim back the 'Promised Land', particularly when the door to it was half-opened for them by the British.

Many consider it unlikely that the Arabs would ever have been able to match the contribution which Israelis have made to the development and prosperity of Palestine. Their pride in the land and their energy cannot be gainsaid. They have literally made the desert bloom.

It is impossible to turn aside, however, from the deprivations suffered by those Palestinians who lost their homes in 1948. When, with UN approval, the Jews claimed the land they had coveted for so long, tens of thousands of settled Arabs became displaced persons, while others now live as second class citizens in modern Israel, many in deplorable conditions in ghettos such as the Jews once knew only too well. Their case is quite simply that they have been deprived of their land and their homes and they want them back. For them there is no such thing as Eretz Israel. The Mosque of Jerusalem, from which they say the Prophet ascended to heaven, is the symbol of their ancient and ordained heritage.

As for the Jews, they argue just as emphatically that the Kingdom of David and the Promised Land are their just inheritance. 'This is our homeland', they say. 'All western culture knows that this is the land that was fought for by the Israelites, and was won by divine ordinance as recorded in holy scripture'.

It is a brave man who comes between such uncompromising viewpoints. Many of us who saw the struggle between the two factions all those years ago can only wish success to those politicians who have come together in the late 20th century to seek a way forward in compromise and goodwill.

WAR 1914-1918

The story of the 'Eastern' perspective of World War I has been told many times. I outline it here merely to refresh memories and to complete my own picture of events as they affect the Palestine/Israel question.

It would be no exaggeration to say that the story has been hyped, paraphrased and romanticized by some of the best writers in the English language into the irresistible saga of Lawrence of Arabia.

In sober fact, the British in August 1914 waited uneasily upon any possible Turkish move into an alliance with the Central Powers (Germany and Austria/Hungary) against the Entente of Britain, France and Russia. When the expected move came in November, Egypt was immediately put under threat of invasion by Turkish forces based in Palestine. In fact, an invasion was attempted, but was beaten off. After a year of stalemate, Sir Henry McMahon Britain's High Commissioner in Cairo, with Whitehall approval, commenced negotiations with the Emir Hussein bin Ali, Sharif of Mecca. The instrument of that policy was a secret organisation known as the Arab Bureau, set up by the joint intelligence chiefs in London, General Macdonogh and Captain Hall RN, but financed and controlled by the Foreign Office intelligence department under Sir William Tyrrell. Lt Cdr Hogarth, previously Keeper of the Ashmolean Museum at Oxford, was the Bureau's director, and among its early members were Miss Gertrude Bell — the first woman ever to serve as an officer of Military Intelligence — Lt TE Lawrence and Lt CL Woolley who up to the war had worked together as archaeologists at the Hittite site of Carchemish and had carried out for Lord Kitchener in Cairo a last-minute survey of Sinai and southern Palestine.

The Bureau's plot was for the Bedouin tribes of the Hejaz (the part of Arabia where the holy cities of Mecca and Medina are located) to rise against their Turkish overlords. Thus it was hoped (and indeed it eventually came about) to roll up the eastern end of the Central Powers' alliance. But it was not until near the end of the war that the British expeditionary force in Egypt under General Sir Edmund Allenby was able finally to force the Turks back across Sinai and into Palestine. There was the triumphant entry into Jerusalem in December 1917, but the final collapse did not come until September of the following year, when Damascus capitulated.

In return for thus assisting the Entente, an agreement was entered into between the Sharif and the High Commissioner, acting for HMG, that defined the frontiers of an independent post-war 'Arabia'. The terms of that agreement, which more-or-less set the boundaries of a post-war Arab Middle East, have always been the subject of heated debate, especially where they affected Palestine.

When it came to the showdown, Britain declared that it was never HMG's intention to include Palestine. But Palestine was clearly included in the wording. It should be added, however, that the agreement with the Sharif was never properly signed or ratified, so that it was not difficult for one British administration to accuse its predecessor of incompetence, and to proceed as if the negotiations had never taken place. It should also be noted, as I wrote at the beginning of this book, that the so-called Sharifian agreement was countermanded by the Sykes-Picot agreement which made Syria a French sphere of influence, Mesopotamia (Iraq) a British sphere, and Palestine an international zone except that its chief port, Haifa, should be under British control. And both those agreements were completely undermined by the Balfour Declaration which, in effect, recognised that Palestine was the legitimate homeland of the Jews. In any case, the Sykes-Picot agreement was divulged very quickly by the Bolsheviks whose first discovery in the archives of the Peterhof was the correspondence of 1916 which allowed Russia to have Constantinople and with it an entrance to the warm waters of the Aegean and Mediterranean. Lenin divulged details of the agreement to the Sharif Husain of Mecca.

As all the world knows, the Emir Faisal, third son of the Sharif Hussein, with Lawrence of British Military Intelligence at his side, took a prominent part in Allenby's victory march into Damascus. Following the exodus of the Turks, the Syrians, with British support, started to form a government. The whole area was garrisoned by the British army as 'OET', Occupied Enemy Territory. The Emir Faisal bin Hussein was installed *de facto* as a constitutional monarch. Following heated debate at the Peace Conference, however, the French argument prevailed, British troops were withdrawn and France

occupied Syria. In July 1920, Faisal was deposed. He later
occupied the throne of the newly created state of Iraq. The
Arabs have always considered that they were the victims
of a British double-cross in regard to the eventual government of Arab countries in general and the disposal of
Palestine in particular.

THE MANDATE

The Oxford Dictionary defines a Mandate as *a commission
from the League of Nations to administer a territory (The
Mandatory).* It came into use at the Paris Peace
Conference in 1919, and was applied to a number of territories, including Palestine and Transjordan, which were
both administered from Jerusalem by a High Commissioner and a team of officers many of whom had originally been recruited into the Colonial Service.

Throughout the entire period of the Mandate, the administration was in effect walking a political tightrope. The
Jews, interpreting perhaps all too liberally the Balfour
Declaration, saw a half-open door and had no reserva-
tions about walking through it into the Promised Land. In
fact, the wording of the Balfour Declaration had been
discussed and worked over endlessly by the Lloyd George
coalition government and by Lord Rothschild its recipient.
Its entire purport was opposed by some of the world's most
prominent Jews. While debate in Cabinet centred on the
use of the words 'Jewish Race' and 'Jewish People', Edwin
Montagu the anti-Zionist Jew in the Government rounded
up opposition opinion. The distinguished French academic
Joseph Reinach declared: 'Jerusalem belongs to all the
religions. We know its history for three thousand years.
The Jewish Kingdom endured for scarcely five centuries'.
Luigi Luzzatti, an Italian Jew and ex-prime minister
wrote: 'Judaism is not a Nationality but a Religion'. LL
Cohen, Chairman of the Jewish Board of Guardians, told

Montagu, '(This) presupposes that the Jews are a nation, which I deny, and that they are homeless, which implies that in countries where they enjoy religious liberty and the full rights of citizenship, they are separate entities, unidentified with the interests of the nations of which they form part, an implication which I repudiate'. It was the Christian conscience within the British Cabinet, backed by Englishmen such as CP Scott, editor of the *Guardian* and a powerful Zionist voice, which finally gave rise to the declaration, delivered to Lord Rothschild in the name of Foreign Secretary Balfour on 2nd November 1917, viewing 'with favour the establishment in Palestine of a national home for the Jewish people', without prejudice to 'the civil and religious rights of non-Jewish communities in Palestine or the rights and political status enjoyed by Jews in any other country'.

Thirty years later, the state of Israel was established. In the interval, as I have tried to show, British troops and police took the brunt of Jewish incursion and Arab resistance.

Inevitably, immigration quotas came into being; but over and above the quotas, Jews came to Palestine in substantial numbers – usually by night in ancient leaky ships and under shockingly overcrowded conditions. For some while, until it took the matter seriously as a result of vehement Arab protests, the administration found it difficult to combat this illegal immigration.

Sentiment was on the side of the Jews and they had an extremely persuasive spokesman in Dr Chaim Weizmann. Whitehall and the Palestine High Commission were bombarded with demands that they increase immigration quotas.

Arab affairs were represented at this time by Haj Amin el Husseini. (I have spoken about him already, and I can still see him in my mind's eye, courteous, sleek, impeccably dressed in black, and speaking in French to my companion, Edward Blatchford). Near the start of the Mandate he had been appointed by the British to the position of Grand Mufti – or the supreme spiritual leader in Palestine. It was, unfortunately, a transparent and quite unsuccessful effort to keep him quiet.

Haj Amin had been since boyhood an inveterate enemy of the British. Now, thinking (as, with reason, did very many Arabs) that despite the terms of the Balfour Declaration, the rights and privileges of all non-Jews in Palestine would in fact be infringed, he threw all his very formidable influence into the balance on behalf of his co-religionists, the Muslim Arabs.

Mandate soon became a dirty word. Eventually, with a state of anarchy prevailing, Whitehall had had enough, and in May 1948, after giving the required notice, it laid down the Mandate and walked out.

THE BIRTH OF ISRAEL

It was widely believed at the time that with the withdrawal of British security forces, the Jews would be driven into the sea by the combined forces of the Arabs. Indeed there was a convergence of four Arab armies upon Palestine; Egyptians, Syrians, Iraqis, and the well-trained, British-led Arab Legion from Transjordan. However, deployment was slow, ponderous and irresolute, lacking in energetic leadership. Had there been proper co-operation with the Arab Legion, following a concerted plan, the eventual result could not have been in much doubt. The Arab cause must have prevailed. But both Britain and the Arab nations had underestimated the strength of the Zionist forces (I stress the word Zionist because the strength of the Jewish effort lay in the domination of every sector by a strong, militant and highly disciplined Zionist caucus backed by a superior intelligence service that came into being before the First World War).

Throughout the time of the Mandate the Jews had been secretly forming an army – the Haganah – with its spearhead formation, the Palmach. The original nucleus of this dated back to 1915 when Jewish units fought with the British at Gallipoli, and later in the Western Desert. There is no doubt that without that covert army (the nature of which may or may not have been known to the mandatory authorities) and without substantial American aid which came in after the Mandate ended, and without their desperate determination – it was indeed 'neck or nothing', the Jews must have been overwhelmed. But Jewish leadership proved professional and resolute, while the Arabs were divided and militarily incompetent.

The Jews prevailed and the State of Israel was born.

Since the Mandate ended, certain place names came into being which are probably not well understood, for example: *West Bank, Gaza Strip, Golan Heights.*

During the Mandate, Palestine was a single undivided country west of the Jordan, bounded in the north by Syria and Lebanon, in the south by Egyptian Sinai, and to the west by the Mediterranean sea. Nobody ever spoke of the West Bank, Gaza Strip and Golan Heights as separate entities. The Golan in any case belonged to Syria, and the inhabitants of Palestine – both Arabs and Jews – were known as Palestinians.

After 1948, hundreds of thousands of Palestinian Arabs – possibly very many more – were either forcibly evicted from their homes or else considered it wise to emigrate quickly to neighbouring Arab countries. They were doubtless sustained by the hope of an early return after the Jews had been driven into the sea by the converging Arab armies. In their new homes, over the years, substantial numbers have prospered and become integrated. However, in the early stages there was very considerable hardship and a race of embittered 'camp' people grew up who in some territories caused much local animosity; they were often thrown out, and had to move on to other places as far afield as north Africa and the Persian Gulf. Some would argue that those who remained in Israel received the worse deal.

After the initial repulse of the Arab armies and the birth of Israel, the United Nations tried, somewhat ineffectually, to take a hand. Commissions had sat much earlier but all they had managed to do was to recommend that this tiny country be partitioned into Arab and Jewish areas. Many who know something of the country have long regarded Palestine as indivisible on account of its size. However, as I write these words there is talk of a breakthrough in Israeli/Palestinian relations. The Gaza Strip and the West Bank town of Jericho have been granted conditional autonomy as Palestinian enclaves, precursors – it is no doubt hoped – of a return to the divisions agreed by the United Nations General Assembly on 29th November 1947. Basically, that 'recommendation' of the UN involved splitting the land into an Arab state of 4,476 square miles in extent (chiefly on the west bank of the Jordan but including a parcel attached to the north-east corner of Sinai known as the Gaza Strip), and a Jewish state of 5,893 square miles. Jerusalem was to be an internationalized city. Thus, the Arabs who owned 90 per cent of the land would have to give up some 47 percent of their tenure, while the Jews would gain that amount. It was not exactly an equitable arrangement, but it was the best the Arabs could hope for in the circumstances and it is the status quo which moderate Arabs must now be hoping to achieve.

As a result of the UN's deliberations, there came into being a curiously truncated country with the newly designated West Bank and Gaza Strip – both traditionally Arab areas. The West Bank, in fact became a part of the Kingdom of Jordan, *faute de mieux*, because the Arab Legion had been firmly entrenched there since the proclamation of the State of Israel, and nobody seemed anxious to dislodge it. There was another partition calling itself East and West Jerusalem. This particular piece of partition entailed considerable head-scratching, because the city possesses shrines that are Holy to Jews, Muslims and Christians. In the event, the Israelis were left without their 'Wailing' Wall (the remains of the ancient Western Wall of Herod's Temple).

It is not surprising, therefore, that Israel has been in a state of almost perpetual war since the partition. In 1948, the War of Independence; 1953, Sinai, or the Suez disaster, where Israeli forces fought in collaboration with British and French against Egypt – until the whole enterprise was knocked on the head by Russia and America; 1967, the Six Day War when Nasser's Egypt was overwhelmed by a pre-emptive Israeli strike; 1973, the so-called 'War of Ramadan' (or 'Yom Kippur' War) against Egypt and Syria when, through overconfidence and, surprisingly, faulty intelligence, the Israelis were nearly unseated, but re-grouped and fought both Egyptians and Syrians to a point when they were only saved by the intervention of the United Nations. In addition there have been constant guerrilla engagements with Syria in the north and Egypt in the south, until hostilities with Egypt were halted by treaty as a result of courageous statesmanship by President Anwar Sadat of Egypt.

It was after the '67 war that Israel 'ironed out' the indentations formed by the Gaza Strip and the West Bank by occupying and administering them. Jerusalem was made whole by abolishing West and East divisions, and the Golan Heights, which had been Syrian territory and had been used for constant shelling of Kibbutzim in northern Galilee, was occupied by Israel.

Much more recently – endeavouring to combat terrorist incursions – Israel has invaded southern Lebanon and created a 'buffer' zone. Finally in order to accommodate

167

some of the large number of immigrants from Russia, there has been substantial Israeli settlement in the mainly Arab-populated area of the so-called West Bank.

Since the ending of the Mandate there have been two massive waves of immigration. The first Aliyah, early on, involved Sephardim, and they presented a particular problem as they had been living for centuries in Arab countries – very much as second class citizens. Their integration into modern living in Israel was a gigantic task.

The second mass Aliyah has only recently taken place, and is still in progress. It consists chiefly of Russian Jews who since the collapse of Communism have been allowed to leave and take up their prescriptive right to citizenship in Israel. For Jews there is always the wide-open door, plus tremendous determination and improvisation.

What of the Future?

Returning to 'The Holy Land' as I have done on five occasions for brief visits, I have been enormously impressed with Israeli achievements in virtually every field of endeavour. This contrasts quite remarkably with the Palestine of my youth when with limited resources, in face of constant civil unrest, and after long centuries of neglect, the British administrators were trying to give back to the land some of the civilised amenities it had so conspicuously enjoyed in the distant past. The Israelis, I found, were falling over themselves in their efforts to turn this long-neglected land into a modern State, and despite all the difficulties they were succeeding. It is true that the forest of TV masts over ancient Jerusalem strike a discordant note, though not quite as discordant as the aerials among the desert communities of Jordan across the river. And in many places there were large numbers of half-finished buildings. The coastal settlements which now appear to run in an endless suburban ribbon between Tel Aviv and Haifa are not very attractive; they have transformed this coastline since my day, and not I am afraid for the better.

I was sad too to find the once splendid skyline of the Mount of Olives obscured by a mass of concrete buildings.

The Israelis are perpetually looking over their shoulders for would-be aggressors. It is a country that has grown accustomed to living under siege conditions. Every Israeli is a potential soldier. It is an ambivalent place. Although there is tension one can still remark an atmosphere of high endeavour and enterprise. There is fierce patriotism tinged with national paranoia; hope born of real achievement in war and peace; fear born of a long history of persecution.

I suppose that if the outside world admires Israel for one thing more than another, it is for the professionalism of its security forces, demonstrated so ably by its ability to track down its most expertly trained and protected opponents, and by such events as the remarkable Entebbe raid. Military Intelligence, spearheaded by Mossad, has reached a level of expertness that would be hard to equal.

When all is said and done, Israel survives by the largesse of its wealthy co-religionists around the world, particularly in America. I would not like to hazard a guess as to what might happen should this aid dry up. Whatever the rights and wrongs of the past, Israel is a *fait accompli*, and its nationhood cannot now be denied. Nevertheless, the Arabs in the most recent negotiations for a restoration of Palestinian land have shown themselves to be models of patience and good sense. There will have to be concessions, and Israel's problem is increasingly obvious – how and where to make concessions without loss of internal security. Egypt and Jordan have proved admirably stable elements in protracted and heated negotiations. It is to be hoped that the statesmanship that has been shown by both sides, usually in the face of vehement opposition by their own compatriots, will in the end bring stability and purpose to the region that has given birth to three great religions of the world, and which much of mankind looks to as the place of good hope.

EDITOR'S NOTES

page 51 'General', a nickname derived from General Townshend, commander of the British force besieged at Kut al Armara in Mesopotamia.

page 94   Faraday and order to fire. A somewhat different account of this incident is given in Horne, *A Job Well Done*, p191ff.

Appendix
pages 143ff In general I have gone along with the author's account of the early history of Palestine, but in this grey area which stands somewhere been biblical authority and archaeology, I think it wise to include here for the reader's assistance the chronology given by the Western Asiatic Department of the British Museum:

Prehistory : Palaeolithic and Mesolithic remains have been found in Palestine, with increasing settlement in Neolithic and Chalcolithic periods.

Early Bronze Age c3100-2200 BC : urban life well established, probable that it included 'Semitic speakers'.

Early Bronze – Middle Bronze c2200-1950 BC : Nomadic incursions. Nomads from eastern steppe, probably included Semitic speaking Amorites. Rock cut tombs of Jericho date from this time.

Canaanite Period, Middle – Late Bronze c1950-1200 : population returned to urban existence soon after 2000 BC and established civilization which lasted until c1200. Early part of this period known as time of Patriarchs, OT. Small groups of non-Canaanite peoples include Hurrians and Indo-Europeans. Egypt dominant power in region; pharaohs of Hyksos and New Kingdom.

End of Bronze Age : marked by major migrations. Raiders, apparently from Aegean, known as 'Sea Peoples', invaded lands of east Mediterranean, one group, Philistines, settling on coast of Palestine. Israelites arrived from Egypt in 13th century BC. Their conquest of Palestine 'can be connected with destruction levels in several cities, notably Hazor'.

Israelite Period c1200 – 597BC: unified Israelite monarchy established by David about 1000BC. Divided on death of his son Solomon in about 922 BC into the two kingdoms of Israel (in north) and Judah (in south). Israel became part of Assyrian Empire in 722BC. Judah remained independent but fell to Babylonians in 597BC. Jerusalem sacked finally in 587/6.

Neo-Babylonian and Persian Periods 597 – 332BC: Cyrus took Babylon in 539BC and permitted return of exiled Jews to Palestine.

Hellenistic and Roman Periods 332BC – 395AD: conquered by Alexander in 332BC. Ruled by Ptolemies from Egypt until 198 BC, then by Seleucids of Syria. After 167, Maccabees and successors liberated increasing area around Judaea. Jewish territory made Roman protectorate by Pompey in 63BC, annexed to Roman Empire in AD6.

Byzantine Period AD395 – 640 : Imperial capital transferred from Rome to Constantinople in AD330. Christianity established as state religion under Theodosius in AD380.

SELECT BIBLIOGRAPHY

Antonius, George, *The Arab Awakening*, London 1979
Avi, Yonah, *The Jews of Palestine*, Oxford 1976
Black, M, and Rowley, HH, (eds), *Pcake's Commentary on the Bible*, London 1962
Buchan, John, *Augustus*, London 1937
Churchill, Winston, *The World Crisis*, (abridged), London 1943
Collins, L, and Lapierre, D, *O Jerusalem*, London 1972
Eban, Abba, *An Autobiography*, London, 1977
Elom, Amos, *The Israelis: Founders and Sons*, New York 1971
Epstein, Isidor, *Judaism*, London 1951
Erskine, Beatrice, *Palestine of the Arabs*, London 1935
Feughwanger, Leon, *Josephus*, London 1932
Fromkin, David, *A Peace to End all Peace*, London 1989
Gibbon, Edward, *Decline and Fall of the Roman Empire* (6 vols), London 1845
Glick, EB, *Between Israel and Death*, London 1974
Glubb, Gen Sir John, *The Story of the Arab Legion*, London 1948
——————— *A Soldier with the Arabs*, London 1957
——————— *Britain and the Arabs*, London 1959
——————— *War in the Desert*, London 1960
——————— *The Empire of the Arabs* London 1963
——————— *Peace in the Holy Land*, London 1971
Grant, Michael, *Herod the Great*, London 1971
Hadawi, Sami, *Bitter Harvest*, Palestine beteen 1914–1967, New York 1967
Heaton, EW, *A History of the Old Testament Prophets*, London 1958
Heikel, Mohammed, *The Road to Ramadan*, London 1975
Hirst, David, *The Gun and the Olive Branch*, London 1977
Horne, Edward P, *A Job Well Done*, Leigh-on-Sea 1982
Johnson Paul, *A History of the Jews*, London 1987
Josephus Flavius, *The Jewish War*, Trnsl. GA Williamson, London 1959

Kaufman, G, *To Build the Promised Land*, London 1974
Keller, Werner, *The Bible as History*, London 1956
Kellett, EE, *A Short History of Religion*, London 1957
Kiernan, T, *Yasir Arafat*, London 1976
Kinross, Lord, *The Ottoman Centuries*, London 1977
Kollek, Teddy, *For Jerusalem, A Life*, London 1978
Lapping, Brian, *End of Empire*, London 1989
Laquer, Walter, *The Israel / Arab Reader: A documentary history
              of the Middle East Conflict*, London 1969
Lawrence, TE, *Seven Pillars of Wisdom*, London 1935
Lias, G, *Glubb's Legion*, London 1956
Liddell Hart, Sir Basil, *History of the First World War*,
                          London 1930
———————————— *History of the Second World War*,
                          London 1970
———————————— *T E Lawrence*, London 1934
Mansfield, Peter, *The Arabs, London* 1976
Meinertzhagen, Richard, *Middle East Diary*, London 1959
Meir, Golda, *My Life*, London 1975
Morton, G, *Just the Job*, London 1957
Nutting, Anthony, *The Arabs*, London 1964
Parkes, James, *A History of the Jewish People*, London 1964
Patai, R, and Patai, J., *The Myth of the Jewish Race*,
                          Detroit 1989
Rice, Michael, *False Inheritance*, London 1994
Rodinson, Maxime, *The Arabs*, London 1981
Stewart, Donald, *Theodor Hertzl*, London 1974
Sachar, Howard, *A History of Israel from the Rise of Zionism
                 to our Time*, Oxford 1976
Storrs, Sir Ronald, *Orientations*, London 1937
Tuchman, Barbara, *Bible and Sword: How the British Came
to Palestine*, London 1982
Wavell, AP, *The Palestine Campaigns*, London 1928
——————— *Allenby, Soldier and Statesman*, London 1974
Williamson, GA, *The World of Josephus*, London 1964
Winstone, HVF, *Gertrude Bell*, London 1978
——————— *The Illicit Adventure*, London 1982
——————— *Uncovering the Ancient World*, London 1985
——————— *Woolley of Ur*, London 1990

INDEX

INDEX